TWO BY CALVIN

Two Classics by John Calvin in One Affordable Volume

containing

ON THE CHRISTIAN LIFE

and

OF PRAYER

John Calvin

LUMEN Christian Products®
Elizabethton, Tennessee

John Calvin

John Calvin was an influential French theologian, author, and pastor during the Protestant Reformation. Calvin's writing and preaching provided the seeds for the branch of theology that bears his name.

CONTENTS

ON THE
CHRISTIAN LIFE

CHAPTER 1

THE CHRISTIAN LIFE: SCRIPTURAL EXHORTATIONS

Section 1

WE have said that the object of regeneration is to bring the life of believers into concord and harmony with the righteousness of God, and so confirm the adoption by which they have been received as sons. But although the law comprehends within it that new life by which the image of God is restored in us, yet, as our sluggishness stands greatly in need both of helps and incentives it will be useful to collect out of Scripture a true account of this reformations lest any who have a heartfelt desire of repentance should in their zeal go astray.

Moreover, I am not unaware that, in undertaking to describe the life of the Christian, I am entering on a large and extensive subject, one which, when fully considered in all its parts, is sufficient to fill a large volume. We see the length to which the Fathers in treating of individual virtues extend their exhortations. This they do, not from mere loquaciousness; for whatever be the virtue which you undertake to recommend, your pen is spontaneously led by the copiousness of the matter so to amplify, that you seem not to have discussed it properly if you have not done it at length. My intention, however, in the plan of life which I now propose to give, is not to extend it so far as to treat of each virtue specially, and expatiate in exhortation. This must be sought in the writings of others, and particularly in the Homilies of the Fathers[1]. For me it will be sufficient to point out the method by which a pious man may be taught how to frame his life

---

[1] The French adds, "C'est a dire, sermons populaires:"--that is to say, "popular sermons."

aright, and briefly lay down some universal rule by which he may not improperly regulate his conduct. I shall one day possibly find time for more ample discourse, (or leave others to perform an office for which I am not so fit. I have a natural love of brevity, and, perhaps, any attempt of mine at copiousness would not succeed. Even if I could gain the highest applause by being more prolix, I would scarcely be disposed to attempt it[2],) while the nature of my present work requires me to glance at simple doctrine with as much brevity as possible.

As philosophers have certain definitions of rectitude and honesty, from which they derive particular duties and the whole train of virtues; so in this respect Scripture is not without order, but presents a most beautiful arrangement, one too which is every way much more certain than that of philosophers. The only difference is, that they, under the influence of ambition, constantly affect an exquisite perspicuity of arrangement, which may serve to display their genius, whereas the Spirit of God, teaching without affectation, is not so perpetually observant of exact method, and yet by observing it at times sufficiently intimates that it is not to be neglected.

Section 2

The Scripture system of which we speak aims chiefly at two objects. The former is that the love of righteousness, to which we are by no means naturally inclined, may be instilled and implanted into our minds. The latter is, (see chap. 2,) to prescribe a rule which will prevent us while in the pursuit of righteousness from going astray. It has numerous admirable methods of recommending righteousness[3]. Many have been already pointed out in different parts of this work; but we shall here also briefly advert to some of them. With what better foundation can it begin than by reminding us that we must

---

[2] The passage in brackets is omitted in the French.

[3] The French begins the sentence thus, "Quant est du premier poinct;"
As to the former point.

be holy, because "God is holy?" (Leviticus 19:12; 1 Peter 1:16.) For when we were scattered abroad like lost sheep, wandering through the labyrinth of this world, he brought us back again to his own fold.

When mention is made of our union with God, let us remember that holiness must be the bond; not that by the merit of holiness we come into communion with him, (we ought rather first to cleave to him, in order that, pervaded with his holiness, we may follow whither he calls,) but because it greatly concerns his glory not to have any fellowship with wickedness and impurity. Wherefore he tells us that this is the end of our calling, the end to which we ought ever to have respect, if we would answer the call of God. For to what end were we rescued from the iniquity and pollution of the world into which we were plunged, if we allow ourselves, during our whole lives, to wallow in them? Besides, we are at the same time admonished, that if we would be regarded as the Lord's people, we must inhabit the holy city Jerusalem, (Isaiah, Revelation 8, etc.) which, as he hath consecrated it to himself, it were impious for its inhabitants to profane by impurity. Hence the expressions, "Who shall abide in thy tabernacle? Who shall dwell in thy holy hill? He that walketh uprightly, and worketh righteousness," (Psalm 15:1, 2; 24:3, 4) for the sanctuary in which he dwells certainly ought not to be like an unclean stall.

Section 3

The better to arouse us, it exhibits God the Father, who, as he hath reconciled us to himself in his Anointed, has impressed his image upon us, to which he would have us to be conformed, (Romans 5:4.) Come, then, and let them show me a more excellent system among philosophers, who think that they only have a moral philosophy duly and orderly arranged. They, when they would give excellent exhortations to virtue, can only tell us to live agreeably to nature.

Scripture derives its exhortations from the true source[4], when it not only enjoins us to regulate our lives with a view to God its author to whom it belongs; but after showing us that we have degenerated from our true origin, viz., the law of our Creator, adds, that Christ, through whom we have returned to favor with God, is set before us as a model, the image of which our lives should express. What do you require more effectual than this? Nay, what do you require beyond this? If the Lord adopts us for his sons on the condition that our life be a representation of Christ, the bond of our adoption,--then, unless we dedicate and devote ourselves to righteousness, we not only, with the utmost perfidy, revolt from our Creator, but also abjure the Savior himself. Then, from an enumeration of all the blessings of God, and each part of our salvation, it finds materials for exhortation.

Ever since God exhibited himself to us as a Father, we must be convicted of extreme ingratitude if we do not in turn exhibit ourselves as his sons. Ever since Christ purified us by the laver of his blood, and communicated this purification by baptism, it would ill become us to be defiled with new pollution. Ever since he engrafted us into his body, we, who are his members, should anxiously beware of contracting any stain or taint. Ever since he who is our head ascended to heaven, it is befitting in us to withdraw our affections from the earth, and with our whole soul aspire to heaven. Ever since the Holy Spirit dedicated us as temples to the Lord, we should make it our endeavor to show forth the glory of God, and guard against being profaned by the defilement of sin. Ever since our soul and body were destined to heavenly incorruptibility and an unfading crown, we should earnestly strive to keep them pure and uncorrupted against the day of the Lord. These, I say, are the surest foundations of a well-regulated life, and you will search in vain for anything resembling them among philosophers, who, in their commendation of virtue, never rise higher than the natural dignity of man.

---

[4] Mal. 1:6; Eph. 5:1; 1 John 3:1, 3; Eph. 5:26; Rom. 6:1-4; 1 Cor. 6:11; 1 Pet. 1:15, 19; 1 Cor. 6:15; John 15:3; Eph. 5:2, 3; Col. 3:1, 2; 1 Cor. 3:16; 6:17; 2 Cor.6:16; 1 Thess. 5:23.

Section 4

This is the place to address those who, having nothing of Christ but the name and sign would yet be called Christians. How dare they boast of this sacred name? None have intercourse with Christ but those who have acquired the true knowledge of him from the Gospel. The Apostle denies that any man truly has learned Christ who has not learned to put off "the old man, which is corrupt according to the deceitful lusts, and put on Christ," (Ephesians 4:22.) They are convicted, therefore, of falsely and unjustly pretending a knowledge of Christ, whatever be the volubility and eloquence with which they can talk of the Gospel.

Doctrine is not an affair of the tongue, but of the life; is not apprehended by the intellect and memory merely, like other branches of learning; but is received only when it possesses the whole soul, and finds its seat and habitation in the inmost recesses of the heart. Let them, therefore, either cease to insult God, by boasting that they are what they are not, or let them show themselves not unworthy disciples of their divine Master. To doctrine in which our religion is contained we have given the first place, since by it our salvation commences; but it must be transfused into the breast, and pass into the conduct, and so transform us into itself, as not to prove unfruitful.

If philosophers are justly offended, and banish from their company with disgrace those who, while professing an art which ought to be the mistress of their conduct, convert it into mere loquacious sophistry, with how much better reason shall we detest those flimsy sophists who are contented to let the Gospel play upon their lips, when, from its efficacy, it ought to penetrate the inmost affections of the heart, fix its seat in the soul, and pervade the whole man a hundred times more than the frigid discourses of philosophers?

Section 5

I insist not that the life of the Christian shall breathe nothing but the perfect Gospel, though this is to be desired, and ought to be attempted. I insist not so strictly on evangelical perfection, as to refuse to acknowledge as a Christian any man who has not attained it. In this way all would be excluded from the Church, since there is no man who is not far removed from this perfection, while many, who have made but little progress, would be undeservedly rejected. What then? Let us set this before our eye as the end at which we ought constantly to aim. Let it be regarded as the goal towards which we are to run. For you cannot divide the matter with God, undertaking part of what his word enjoins, and omitting part at pleasure.

For, in the first place, God uniformly recommends integrity as the principal part of his worship, meaning by integrity real singleness of mind, devoid of gloss and fiction, and to this is opposed a double mind; as if it had been said, that the spiritual commencement of a good life is when the internal affections are sincerely devoted to God, in the cultivation of holiness and justice. But seeing that, in this earthly prison of the body, no man is supplied with strength sufficient to hasten in his course with due alacrity, while the greater number are so oppressed with weakness, that hesitating, and halting, and even crawling on the ground, they make little progress, let every one of us go as far as his humble ability enables him, and prosecute the journey once begun. No one will travel so badly as not daily to make some degree of progress. This, therefore, let us never cease to do, that we may daily advance in the way of the Lord; and let us not despair because of the slender measure of success. How little soever the success may correspond with our wish, our labor is not lost when to-day is better than yesterday, provided with true singleness of mind we keep our aim, and aspire to the goal, not speaking flattering things to ourselves, nor indulging our vices, but making it our constant endeavor to become better, until we attain to goodness itself. If during the whole course of our life we seek and follow, we shall at length attain it, when relieved from the infirmity of flesh we are admitted to full fellowship with God.

CHAPTER 2

A SUMMARY OF THE CHRISTIAN LIFE: SELF-DENIAL[5]

Section 1

ALTHOUGH the Law of God contains a perfect rule of conduct admirably arranged, it has seemed proper to our divine Master to train his people by a more accurate method, to the rule which is enjoined in the Law; and the leading principle in the method is, that it is the duty of believers to present their "bodies a living sacrifice, holy and acceptable unto God, which is their reasonable service," (Romans 12:1.) Hence he draws the exhortation: "Be not conformed to this world: but be ye transformed by the renewing of your mind, that ye may prove what is that good, and acceptable, and perfect will of God." The great point, then, is, that we are consecrated and dedicated to God, and, therefore, should not henceforth think, speak, design, or act, without a view to his glory. What he hath made sacred cannot, without signal insult to him, be applied to profane use.

But if we are not our own, but the Lord's, it is plain both what error is to be shunned, and to what end the actions of our lives ought to be directed. We are not our own; therefore, neither is our own reason or will to rule our acts and counsels. We are not our own; therefore, let us not make it our end to seek what may be agreeable to our carnal nature. We are not our own; therefore, as far as possible, let us forget ourselves and the things that are ours. On the other hand, we are God's; let us, therefore, live and die to him (Romans 14:8.) We are

---

[5] On this and the three following chapters, which contain the second part of the Treatise on the Christian Life, see Augustine, *De Moribus Ecclesiae Catholicae*, and *Calvin de Scandalis*.

God's; therefore, let his wisdom and will preside over all our actions. We are God's; to him, then, as the only legitimate end, let every part of our life be directed. O how great the proficiency of him who, taught that he is not his own, has withdrawn the dominion and government of himself from his own reason that he may give them to God! For as the surest source of destruction to men is to obey themselves, so the only haven of safety is to have no other will, no other wisdom, than to follow the Lord wherever he leads.

Let this, then be the first step, to abandon ourselves, and devote the whole energy of our minds to the service of God. By service, I mean not only that which consists in verbal obedience, but that by which the mind, divested of its own carnal feelings, implicitly obeys the call of the Spirit of God. This transformation, (which Paul calls the renewing of the mind, Romans 12:2; Ephesians4:23.) though it is the first entrance to life, was unknown to all the philosophers. They give the government of man to reason alone, thinking that she alone is to be listened to; in short, they assign to her the sole direction of the conduct. But Christian philosophy bids her give place, and yield complete submission to the Holy Spirit, so that the man himself no longer lives, but Christ lives and reigns in him, (Galatians 2:20.)

Section 2

Hence follows the other principle, that we are not to seek our own, but the Lord's will, and act with a view to promote his glory. Great is our proficiency, when, almost forgetting ourselves, certainly postponing our own reason, we faithfully make it our study to obey God and his commandments. For when Scripture enjoins us to lay aside private regard to ourselves, it not only divests our minds of an excessive longing for wealth, or power, or human favor, but eradicates all ambition and thirst for worldly glory, and other more secret pests.

The Christian ought, indeed, to be so trained and disposed as to consider, that during his whole life he has to do with God. For this reason, as he will bring all things to the disposal and estimate of God, so he will religiously direct his whole mind to him. For he who has learned to look to God in everything he does, is at the same time diverted from all vain thoughts. This is that self-denial which Christ so strongly enforces on his disciples from the very outset, (Matthew 16:24,) which, as soon as it takes hold of the mind, leaves no place either, first, for pride, show, and ostentation; or, secondly, for avarice, lust, luxury, effeminacy, or other vices which are engendered by self love.

On the contrary, wherever it reigns not, the foulest vices are indulged in without shame; or, if there is some appearance of virtue, it is vitiated by a depraved longing for applause. Show me, if you can, an individual who, unless he has renounced himself in obedience to the Lord's command, is disposed to do good for its own sake. Those who have not so renounced themselves have followed virtue at least for the sake of praise. The philosophers who have contended most strongly that virtue is to be desired on her own account, were so inflated with arrogance as to make it apparent that they sought virtue for no other reason than as a ground for indulging in pride. So far, therefore, is God from being delighted with these hunters after popular applause with their swollen breasts, that he declares they have received their reward in this world, (Matthew 6:2,) and that harlots and publicans are nearer the kingdom of heaven than they, (Matthew 21:31.) We have not yet sufficiently explained how great and numerous are the obstacles by which a man is impeded in the pursuit of rectitude, so long as he has not renounced himself.

The old saying is true, There is a world of iniquity treasured up in the human soul. Nor can you find any other remedy for this than to deny yourself, renounce your own reason, and direct your whole mind to the pursuit of those things which the Lord requires of you, and which you are to seek only because they are pleasing to Him.

Section 3

In another passage, Paul gives a brief, indeed, but more distinct account of each of the parts of a well-ordered life: "The grace of God that bringeth salvation hath appeared to all men, teaching us that, denying ungodliness and worldly lusts, we should live soberly, righteously, and godly, in this present world; looking for that blessed hope, and the glorious appearance of the great God and our Savior Jesus Christ; who gave himself for us, that he might redeem us from all iniquity, and purify to himself a peculiar people, zealous of good works," (Titus 2:11-14.) After holding forth the grace of God to animate us, and pave the way for His true worship, he removes the two greatest obstacles which stand in the way, viz., ungodliness, to which we are by nature too prone, and worldly lusts, which are of still greater extent. Under ungodliness, he includes not merely superstition, but everything at variance with the true fear of God. Worldly lusts are equivalent to the lusts of the flesh.

Thus he enjoins us, in regard to both tables of the Law, to lay aside our own mind, and renounce whatever our own reason and will dictate. Then he reduces all the actions of our lives to three branches, sobriety, righteousness, and godliness. Sobriety undoubtedly denotes as well chastity and temperance as the pure and frugal use of temporal goods, and patient endurance of want. Righteousness comprehends all the duties of equity, in every one his due. Next follows godliness, which separates us from the pollutions of the world, and connects us with God in true holiness. These, when connected together by an indissoluble chain, constitute complete perfection. But as nothing is more difficult than to bid adieu to the will of the flesh, subdue, nay, abjure our lusts, devote ourselves to God and our brethren, and lead an angelic life amid the pollutions of the world, Paul, to set our minds free from all entanglements, recalls us to the hope of a blessed immortality, justly urging us to contend, because as Christ has once appeared as our Redeemer, so on his final advent he will give full effect to the salvation obtained by him. And in this way he dispels all the allurements which becloud our path, and prevent us from aspiring as we ought to heavenly glory; nay, he tells us that we must be pilgrims in the world, that we may not fail of obtaining the heavenly inheritance.

Section 4

Moreover, we see by these words that self-denial has respect partly to men and partly (more especially) to God. For when Scripture enjoins us, in regard to our fellow men, to prefer them in honor to ourselves, and sincerely labor to promote their advantages (Romans 12:10; Philippians 2:3), he gives us commands which our mind is utterly incapable of obeying until its natural feelings are suppressed. For so blindly do we all rush in the direction of self-love, that everyone thinks he has a good reason for exalting himself and despising all others in comparison. If God has bestowed on us something not to be repented of, trusting to it, we immediately become elated, and not only swell, but almost burst with pride. The vices with which we abound we both carefully conceal from others, and flatteringly represent to ourselves as minute and trivial, nay, sometimes hug them as virtues. When the same qualities which we admire in ourselves are seen in others, even though they should be superior, we, in order that we may not be forced to yield to them, maliciously lower and carp at them; in like manner, in the case of vices, not contented with severe and keen animadversion, we studiously exaggerate them.

Hence the insolence with which each, as if exempted from the common lot, seeks to exalt himself above his neighbor, confidently and proudly despising others, or at least looking down upon them as his inferiors. The poor man yields to the rich, the plebeian to the noble, the servant to the master, the unlearned to the learned, and yet every one inwardly cherishes some idea of his own superiority. Thus each flattering himself, sets up a kind of kingdom in his breast; the arrogant, to satisfy themselves, pass censure on the minds and manners of other men, and when contention arises, the full venom is displayed. Many bear about with them some measure of mildness so long as all things go smoothly and lovingly with them, but how few are there who, when stung and irritated, preserve the same tenor of moderation? For this there is no other remedy than to pluck up by the roots those most noxious pests, self-love and love of victory. This the doctrine of Scripture does. For it teaches us to remember, that the endowments which God has bestowed upon us are not our own, but His free gifts, and that those who plume themselves upon them betray their ingratitude. "Who maketh thee to differ," saith Paul, "and what hast thou that thou didst not receive? now if thou didst receive it, why dost thou glory, as if thou hadst not received it?" (1 Corinthians 4:7.) Then by a diligent examination of our faults let us keep ourselves humble.

Thus while nothing will remain to swell our pride, there will be much to subdue it. Again, we are enjoined, whenever we behold the gifts of God in others, so to reverence and respect the gifts, as also to honor those in whom they reside. God having been pleased to bestow honor upon them, it would ill become us to deprive them of it. Then we are told to overlook their faults, not, indeed, to encourage by flattering them, but not because of them to insult those whom we ought to regard with honor and good will[6].

In this way, with regard to all with whom we have intercourse, our behavior will be not only moderate and modest, but courteous and friendly. The only way by which you can ever attain to true meekness, is to have your heart imbued with a humble opinion of yourself and respect for others.

Section 5

How difficult it is to perform the duty of seeking the good of our neighbor! Unless you leave off all thought of yourself and in a manner cease to be yourself, you will never accomplish it. How can you exhibit those works of charity which Paul describes unless you renounce yourself, and become wholly devoted to others? "Charity (says he, 1 Corinthians 13:4) suffereth long, and is kind; charity envieth not; charity vaunteth not itself, is not puffed up, doth not behave itself unseemly, seeketh not her own, is not easily provoked etc." Were it

---

[6] Calvin. *de Sacerdotiis Eccles. Papal.* in fine.

the only thing required of us to seek not our own, nature would not have the least power to comply: she so inclines us to love ourselves only, that she will not easily allow us carelessly to pass by ourselves and our own interests that we may watch over the interests of others, nay, spontaneously to yield our own rights and resign it to another.

But Scripture, to conduct us to this, reminds us, that whatever we obtain from the Lord is granted on the condition of our employing it for the common good of the Church, and that, therefore, the legitimate use of all our gifts is a kind and liberal communication of them with others. There cannot be a surer rule, nor a stronger exhortation to the observance of it, than when we are taught that all the endowments which we possess are divine deposits entrusted to us for the very purpose of being distributed for the good of our neighbor.

But Scripture proceeds still farther when it likens these endowments to the different members of the body, (1 Corinthians 12:12.) No member has its function for itself, or applies it for its own private use, but transfers it to its fellow-members; nor does it derive any other advantage from it than that which it receives in common with the whole body. Thus, whatever the pious man can do, he is bound to do for his brethren, not consulting his own interest in any other way than by striving earnestly for the common edification of the Church. Let this, then, be our method of showing good-will and kindness, considering that, in regard to everything which God has bestowed upon us, and by which we can aid our neighbor, we are his stewards, and are bound to give account of our stewardship; moreover, that the only right mode of administration is that which is regulated by love. In this way, we shall not only unite the study of our neighbor's advantage with a regard to our own, but make the latter subordinate to the former.

And lest we should have omitted to perceive that this is the law for duly administering every gift which we receive from God, he of old applied that law to the minutest expressions of his own kindness. He commanded the first-fruits to be offered to him as an attestation by the people that it was impious to reap any advantage from goods not previously consecrated to him, (Exodus 22:29; 23:19.) But if the gifts of God are not sanctified to us until we have with our own hand dedicated them to the Giver, it must be a gross abuse that does not give signs of such dedication. It is in vain to contend that you cannot enrich the Lord by your offerings. Though, as the Psalmist says "Thou art my Lord: my goodness extendeth not unto thee," yet you can extend it "to the saints that are in the earth," (Psalm 16:2, 3); and therefore a comparison is drawn between sacred oblations and alms as now corresponding to the offerings under the Law. (Hebrews 12:16; 2 Corinthians 9:12).

Section 6

Moreover, that we may not weary in well-doing, (as would otherwise forthwith and infallibly be the case,) we must add the other quality in the Apostle's enumeration, "Charity suffereth long, and is kind, is not easily provoked," (1 Corinthians 13:4.) The Lord enjoins us to do good to all without exception, though the greater part, if estimated by their own merit, are most unworthy of it.

But Scripture subjoins a most excellent reason, when it tells us that we are not to look to what men in themselves deserve, but to attend to the image of God, which exists in all, and to which we owe all honor and love. But in those who are of the household of faith, the same rule is to be more carefully observed, inasmuch as that image is renewed and restored in them by the Spirit of Christ. Therefore, whoever be the man that is presented to you as needing your assistance, you have no ground for declining to give it to him. Say he is a stranger. The Lord has given him a mark which ought to be familiar to you: for which reason he forbids you to despise your own flesh, (Galatians 6:10.) Say he is mean and of no consideration. The Lord points him out as one whom he has distinguished by the luster of his own image, (Isaiah 58:7.) Say that you are bound to him by no ties of duty. The Lord has substituted him as it were into his own place, that in him you may recognize the many great obligations under which the Lord has laid you to himself. Say that he is unworthy of your least exertion on his account; but the image of God, by which he is recommended to you, is worthy of yourself and all your exertions. But if he not only merits no good, but has provoked you by injury and mischief, still this is no good reason why you should not embrace him in love, and visit him with offices of love.

He has deserved very differently from me, you will say. But what has the Lord deserved?[7] Whatever injury he has done you, when he enjoins you to forgive him, he certainly means that it should be imputed to himself. In this way only we attain to what is not to say difficult but altogether against nature, (Matthew 5:44; 6:14; 18:35; Luke 17:3) to love those that hate us, render good for evil, and blessing for cursing, remembering that we are not to reflect on the wickedness of men, but look to the image of God in them, an image which, covering and obliterating their faults, should by its beauty and dignity allure us to love and embrace them.

Section 7

We shall thus succeed in mortifying ourselves if we fulfill all the duties of charity. Those duties, however, are not fulfilled by the mere discharge of them, though none be omitted, unless it is done from a pure feeling of love. For it may happen that one may perform every one of these offices, in so far as the external act is concerned, and be far from performing them aright. For you see some who would be thought very liberal, and yet accompany everything they give with insult, by the haughtiness of their looks, or the violence of their words.

---

[7] French, "Car si nous disons qu'il n'a merité que mal de nous; Dieu nous pourra demander quel mal il nous a fait, lui dont nous tenons tout notre bien;"--For if we say that he has deserved nothing of us but evil, God may ask us what evil he has done us, he of whom we hold our every blessing.

And to such a calamitous condition have we come in this unhappy age, that the greater part of men never almost give alms without contumely.

Such conduct ought not to have been tolerated even among the heathen; but from Christians something more is required than to carry cheerfulness in their looks, and give attractiveness to the discharge of their duties by courteous language. First, they should put themselves in the place of him whom they see in need of their assistance, and pity his misfortune as if they felt and bore it, so that a feeling of pity and humanity should incline them to assist him just as they would themselves. He who is thus minded will go and give assistance to his brethren, and not only not taint his acts with arrogance or upbraiding but will neither look down upon the brother to whom he does a kindness, as one who needed his help, or keep him in subjection as under obligation to him, just as we do not insult a diseased member when the rest of the body labors for its recovery, nor think it under special obligation to the other members, because it has required more exertion than it has returned. A communication of offices between members is not regarded as at all gratuitous, but rather as the payment of that which being due by the law of nature it were monstrous to deny.

For this reason, he who has performed one kind of duty will not think himself thereby discharged, as is usually the case when a rich man, after contributing somewhat of his substance, delegates remaining burdens to others as if he had nothing to do with them. Everyone should rather consider, that however great he is, he owes himself to his neighbors, and that the only limit to his beneficence is the failure of his means. The extent of these should regulate that of his charity.

Section 8

The principal part of self-denial, that which as we have said has reference to God, let us again consider more fully. Many things have already been said with regard to it which it were superfluous to repeat; and, therefore, it will be sufficient to view it as forming us to equanimity and endurance. First, then, in seeking the convenience or tranquility of the present life, Scripture calls us to resign ourselves, and all we have, to the disposal of the Lord, to give him up the affections of our heart, that he may tame and subdue them. We have a frenzied desire, an infinite eagerness, to pursue wealth and honor, intrigue for power, accumulate riches, and collect all those frivolities which seem conducive to luxury and splendor.

On the other hand, we have a remarkable dread, a remarkable hatred of poverty, mean birth, and a humble condition, and feel the strongest desire to guard against them. Hence, in regard to those who frame their life after their own counsel, we see how restless they are in mind, how many plans they try, to what fatigues they submit, in order that they may gain what avarice or ambition desires, or, on the other hand, escape poverty and meanness. To avoid similar entanglements, the course which Christian men must follow is this: first, they must not long for, or hope for, or think of any kind of prosperity apart from the blessing of God; on it they must cast themselves, and there safely and confidently recline. For, however much the carnal mind may seem sufficient for itself when in the pursuit of honor or wealth, it depends on its own industry and zeal, or is aided by the favor of men, it is certain that all this is nothing, and that neither intellect nor labor will be of the least avail, except in so far as the Lord prospers both.

On the contrary, his blessing alone makes a way through all obstacles, and brings everything to a joyful and favorable issue. Secondly, though without this blessing we may be able to acquire some degree of fame and opulence, (as we daily see wicked men loaded with honors and riches,) yet since those on whom the curse of God lies do not enjoy the least particle of true happiness, whatever we obtain without his blessing must turn out ill. But surely men ought not to desire what adds to their misery.

Section 9

Therefore, if we believe that all prosperous and desirable success depends entirely on the blessing of God, and that when it is wanting all kinds of misery and calamity await us, it follows that we should not eagerly contend for riches and honors, trusting to our own dexterity and assiduity, or leaning on the favor of men, or confiding in any empty imagination of fortune; but should always have respect to the Lord, that under his auspices we may be conducted to whatever lot he has provided for us.

First, the result will be, that instead of rushing on regardless of right and wrong, by wiles and wicked arts, and with injury to our neighbors, to catch at wealth and seize upon honors, we will only follow such fortune as we may enjoy with innocence. Who can hope for the aid of the divine blessing amid fraud, rapine, and other iniquitous arts? As this blessing attends him only who thinks purely and acts uprightly, so it calls off all who long for it from sinister designs and evil actions.

Secondly, a curb will be laid upon us, restraining a too eager desire of becoming rich, or an ambitious striving after honor. How can anyone have the effrontery to expect that God will aid him in accomplishing desires at variance with his word? What God with his own lips pronounces cursed, never can be prosecuted with his blessing.

Lastly, if our success is not equal to our wish and hope, we shall, however, be kept from impatience and detestation of our condition, whatever it be, knowing that so to feel were to murmur against God, at whose pleasure riches and poverty, contempt and honors, are dispensed. In short, he who leans on the divine blessing in the way which has been described, will not, in the pursuit of those things which men are wont most eagerly to desire, employ wicked arts which he knows would avail him nothing; nor when anything prosperous befalls him will he impute it to himself and his own diligence, or industry, or fortune, instead of ascribing it to God as its author. If, while the affairs of others flourish, his make little progress, or even retrograde, he will bear his humble lot with greater equanimity and moderation than any irreligious man does the moderate success which only falls short of what he wished; for he has a solace in which he can rest more tranquilly than at the very summit of wealth or power, because he considers that his affairs are ordered by the Lord in the manner most conducive to his salvation. This, we see, is the way in which David was affected, who, while he follows God and gives up himself to his guidance, declares, "Neither do I exercise myself in great matters, or in things too high for me. Surely I have behaved and quieted myself as a child that is weaned of his mother," (Psalm 131:1, 2).

Section 10

Nor is it in this respect only that pious minds ought to manifest this tranquility and endurance; it must be extended to all the accidents to which this present life is liable. He alone, therefore, has properly denied himself, who has resigned himself entirely to the Lord, placing all the course of his life entirely at his disposal. Happen what may, he whose mind is thus composed will neither deem himself wretched nor murmur against God because of his lot.

How necessary this disposition is will appear, if you consider the many accidents to which we are liable. Various diseases ever and anon attack us: at one time pestilence rages; at another we are involved in all the calamities of war. Frost and hail, destroying the promise of the year, cause sterility, which reduces us to penury; wife, parents, children, relatives, are carried off by death; our house is destroyed by fire. These are the events which make men curse their life, detest the day of their birth, execrate the light of heaven, even censure God, and (as they are eloquent in blasphemy) charge him with cruelty and injustice. The believer must in these things also contemplate the mercy and truly paternal indulgence of God.

Accordingly, should he see his house by the removal of kindred reduced to solitude even then he will not cease to bless the Lord; his thought will be, Still the grace of the Lord, which dwells within my house, will not leave it desolate. If his crops are blasted, mildewed, or cut off by frost, or struck down by hail[8], and he sees famine before him, he will not however despond or murmur against God, but maintain his confidence in him; "We thy people, and sheep of thy pasture, will give thee thanks for ever," (Psalm 79:13;) he will supply me with food, even in the extreme of sterility. If he is afflicted with disease, the sharpness of the pain will not so overcome him, as to make him break out with impatience, and expostulate with God; but, recognizing justice and lenity in the rod, will patiently endure.

In short, whatever happens, knowing that it is ordered by the Lord, he will receive it with a placid and grateful mind, and will not contumaciously resist the government of him, at whose disposal he has placed himself and all that he has. Especially let the Christian breast eschew that foolish and most miserable consolation of the heathen, who, to strengthen their mind against adversity, imputed it to fortune, at which they deemed it absurd to feel indignant, as she was aimless and rash, and blindly wounded the good equally with the bad. On the contrary, the rule of piety is, that the hand of God is the ruler and arbiter of the fortunes of all, and, instead of rushing on with thoughtless violence, dispenses good and evil with perfect regularity.

---

[8] The French is, "Soit que ses bleds et vignes soyent gastées et destruites par gelée, gresle, ou autre tempeste;"--whether his corn and vines are hurt and destroyed by frost, hail, or other tempest.

CHAPTER 3

OF BEARING THE CROSS-
ONE ASPECT OF SELF-DENIAL

Section 1

THE pious mind must ascend still higher, namely, whither Christ calls his disciples when he says, that every one of them must "take up his cross," (Matthew 16:24.) Those whom the Lord has chosen and honored with his intercourse must prepare for a hard, laborious, troubled life, a life full of many and various kinds of evils; it being the will of our heavenly Father to exercise his people in this way while putting them to the proof. Having begun this course with Christ the first-born, he continues it towards all his children.

For though that Son was dear to him above others, the Son in whom he was "well pleased," yet we see, that far from being treated gently and indulgently, we may say, that not only was he subjected to a perpetual cross while he dwelt on earth, but his whole life was nothing else than a kind of perpetual cross. The Apostle assigns the reason, "Though he was a Son, yet learned he obedience by the things which he suffered," (Hebrews 5:8.) Why then should we exempt ourselves from that condition to which Christ our Head behooved to submit; especially since he submitted on our account, that he might in his own person exhibit a model of patience?

Wherefore, the Apostle declares, that all the children of God are destined to be conformed to him. Hence it affords us great consolation in hard and difficult circumstances, which men deem evil and adverse, to think that we are holding fellowship with the sufferings of Christ; that as he passed to celestial glory through a labyrinth of many woes, so we too are conducted thither through various tribulations. For, in another passage, Paul himself thus speaks, "we must through much tribulation enter the kingdom of God," (Acts 14:22;) and again, "that I may know him, and the power of his resurrection, and the fellowship of his sufferings, being made conformable unto his death," (Romans 8:29.) How powerfully should it soften the bitterness of the cross, to think that the more we are afflicted with adversity, the surer we are made of our fellowship with Christ; by communion with whom our sufferings are not only blessed to us, but tend greatly to the furtherance of our salvation.

Section 2

We may add, that the only thing which made it necessary for our Lord to undertake to bear the cross, was to testify and prove his obedience to the Father; whereas there are many reasons which make it necessary for us to live constantly under the cross. Feeble as we are by nature, and prone to ascribe all perfection to our flesh, unless we receive as it were ocular demonstration of our weakness, we readily estimate our virtue above its proper worth, and doubt not that, whatever happens, it will stand unimpaired and invincible against all difficulties.

Hence we indulge a stupid and empty confidence in the flesh, and then trusting to it wax proud against the Lord himself; as if our own faculties were sufficient without his grace. This arrogance cannot be better repressed than when He proves to us by experience, not only how great our weakness, but also our frailty is. Therefore, he visits us with disgrace, or poverty, or bereavement, or disease, or other afflictions. Feeling altogether unable to support them, we forthwith, in so far as regards ourselves, give way, and thus humbled learn to invoke his strength, which alone can enable us to bear up under a weight of affliction.

Nay, even the holiest of men, however well aware that they stand not in their own strength, but by the grace of God, would feel too secure in their own fortitude and constancy, were they not brought to a more thorough knowledge of themselves by the trial of the cross. This feeling gained even upon David, "In my prosperity I Said, I shall never be moved. Lord, by thy favor thou hast made my mountain to stand strong: thou didst hide thy face, and I was troubled," (Psalm 30:6, 7.) He confesses that in prosperity his feelings were dulled and blunted, so that, neglecting the grace of God, on which alone he ought to have depended, he leant to himself, and promised himself perpetuity. If it so happened to this great prophet, who of us should not fear and study caution? Though in tranquility they flatter themselves with the idea of greater constancy and patience, yet, humbled by adversity, they learn the deception.

Believers, I say, warned by such proofs of their diseases, make progress in humility, and, divesting themselves of a depraved confidence in the flesh, betake themselves to the grace of God, and, when they have so betaken themselves, experience the presence of the divine power, in which is ample protection.

Section 3

This Paul teaches when he says that tribulation worketh patience, and patience experience. God having promised that he will be with believers in tribulation, they feel the truth of the promise; while supported by his hand, they endure patiently. This they could never do by their own strength. Patience, therefore, gives the saints an experimental proof that God in reality furnishes the aid which he has promised whenever there is need.

Hence also their faith is confirmed, for it were very ungrateful not to expect that in future the truth of God will be, as they have already found it, firm and constant. We now see how many advantages are at once produced by the cross. Overturning the overweening opinion we form of our own virtue, and detecting the hypocrisy in which we delight, it removes our pernicious carnal confidence, teaching us, when thus humbled, to recline on God alone, so that we neither are oppressed nor despond. Then victory is followed by hope, inasmuch as the Lord, by performing what he has promised, establishes his truth in regard to the future. Were these the only reasons, it is surely plain how necessary it is for us to bear the cross. It is of no little importance to be rid of your self-love, and made fully conscious of your weakness; so impressed with a sense of your weakness as to learn to distrust yourself--to distrust yourself so as to transfer your confidence to God, reclining on him with such heartfelt confidence as to trust in his aid, and continue invincible to the end, standing by his grace so as to perceive that he is true to his promises, and so assured of the certainty of his promises as to be strong in hope.

Section 4

Another end which the Lord has in afflicting his people is to try their patience, and train them to obedience--not that they can yield obedience to him except in so far as he enables them; but he is pleased thus to attest and display striking proofs of the graces which he has conferred upon his saints, lest they should remain within unseen and unemployed. Accordingly, by bringing forward openly the strength and constancy of endurance with which he has provided his servants, he is said to try their patience. Hence the expressions that God tempted Abraham, (Genesis 21:1, 12,) and made proof of his piety by not declining to sacrifice his only son. Hence, too, Peter tells us that our faith is proved by tribulation, just as gold is tried in a furnace of fire. But who will say it is not expedient that the most excellent gift of patience which the believer has received from his God should be applied to uses by being made sure and manifest? Otherwise men would never value it according to its worth.

But if God himself, to prevent the virtues which he has conferred upon believers from lurking in obscurity, nay, lying useless and perishing, does aright in supplying materials for calling them forth, there is the best reason for the afflictions of the saints, since without them their patience could not exist. I say, that by the cross they are also trained to obedience, because they are thus taught to live not according to their own wish, but at the disposal of God. Indeed, did all things proceed as they wish, they would not know what it is to follow God. Seneca mentions (*De Vita Beata*, book 15) that there was an old proverb when any one was exhorted to endure adversity, "Follow God;" thereby intimating, that men truly submitted to the yoke of God only when they gave their back and hand to his rod. But if it is most right that we should in all things prove our obedience to our heavenly Father, certainly we ought not to decline any method by which he trains us to obedience.

Section 5

Still, however, we see not how necessary that obedience is, unless we at the same time consider how prone our carnal nature is to shake off the yoke of God whenever it has been treated with some degree of gentleness and indulgence. It just happens to it as with refractory horses, which, if kept idle for a few days at hack and manger, become ungovernable, and no longer recognize the rider, whose command before they implicitly obeyed. And we invariably become what God complains of in the people of Israel--waxing gross and fat, we kick against him who reared and nursed us, (Deuteronomy 32:15.)

The kindness of God should allure us to ponder and love his goodness; but since such is our malignity, that we are invariably corrupted by his indulgence, it is more than necessary for us to be restrained by discipline from breaking forth into such petulance. Thus, lest we become emboldened by an over-abundance of wealth; lest elated with honor, we grow proud; lest inflated with other advantages of body, or mind, or fortune, we grow insolent, the Lord himself interferes as he sees to be expedient by means of the cross, subduing and curbing the arrogance of our flesh, and that in various ways, as the advantage of each requires. For as we do not all equally labor under the same disease, so we do not all need the same difficult cure. Hence we see that all are not exercised with the same kind of cross.

While the heavenly Physician treats some more gently, in the case of others he employs harsher remedies, his purpose being to provide a cure for all. Still none is left free and untouched, because he knows that all, without a single exception, are diseased.

Section 6

We may add, that our most merciful Father requires not only to prevent our weakness, but often to correct our past faults, that he may keep us in due obedience. Therefore, whenever we are afflicted we ought immediately to call to mind our past life. In this way we will find that the faults which we have committed are deserving of such castigation. And yet the exhortation to patience is not to be founded chiefly on the acknowledgment of sin. For Scripture supplies a far better consideration when it says, that in adversity "we are chastened of the Lord, that we should not be condemned with the world," (1 Corinthians 11:32.)

Therefore, in the very bitterness of tribulation we ought to recognize the kindness and mercy of our Father, since even then he ceases not to further our salvation. For he afflicts, not that he may ruin or destroy but rather that he may deliver us from the condemnation of the world. Let this thought lead us to what Scripture elsewhere teaches: "My son, despise not the chastening of the Lord; neither be weary of his correction: For whom the Lord loveth he correcteth; even as a father the son in whom he delighteth," (Proverbs 3:11, 12.) When we perceive our Father's rod, is it not our part to behave as obedient docile sons rather than rebelliously imitate desperate men, who are hardened in wickedness? God dooms us to destruction, if he does not, by correction, call us back when we have fallen off from him, so that it is truly said, "If ye be without chastisement," "then are ye bastards, and not sons," (Hebrews 12:8.)

We are most perverse then if we cannot bear him while he is manifesting his good-will to us, and the care which he takes of our salvation. Scripture states the difference between believers and unbelievers to be, that the latter, as the slaves of inveterate and deep-seated iniquity, only become worse and more obstinate under the lash; whereas the former, like free-born sons turn to repentance. Now, therefore, choose your class. But as I have already spoken of this subject, it is sufficient to have here briefly adverted to it.

Section 7

There is singular consolation, moreover, when we are persecuted for righteousness' sake. For our thought should then be, How high the honor which God bestows upon us in distinguishing us by the special badge of his soldiers. By suffering persecution for righteousness' sake, I mean not only striving for the defense of the Gospel, but for the defense of righteousness in any way. Whether, therefore, in maintaining the truth of God against the lies of Satan, or defending the good and innocent against the injuries of the bad, we are obliged to incur the offence and hatred of the world, so as to endanger life, fortune, or honor, let us not grieve or decline so far to spend ourselves for God; let us not think ourselves wretched in those things in which he with his own lips has pronounced us blessed, (Matthew 5:10.) Poverty, indeed considered in itself, is misery; so are exile, contempt, imprisonment, ignominy: in fine, death itself is the last of all calamities.

But when the favor of God breathes upon is, there is none of these things which may not turn out to our happiness. Let us then be contented with the testimony of Christ rather than with the false estimate of the flesh, and then, after the example of the Apostles, we will rejoice in being "counted worthy to suffer shame for his name," (Acts 5:41.) For why? If, while conscious of our innocence, we are deprived of our substance by the wickedness of man, we are, no doubt, humanly speaking, reduced to poverty; but in truth our riches in heaven are increased: if driven from our homes we have a more welcome reception into the family of God; if vexed and despised, we are more firmly rooted in Christ; if stigmatized by disgrace and ignominy, we have a higher place in the kingdom of God; and if we are slain, entrance is thereby given us to eternal life. The Lord having set such a price upon us, let us be ashamed to estimate ourselves at less than the shadowy and evanescent allurements of the present life.

Section 8

Since by these, and similar considerations, Scripture abundantly solaces us for the ignominy or calamities which we endure in defense of righteousness, we are very ungrateful if we do not willingly and cheerfully receive them at the hand of the Lord, especially since this form of the cross is the most appropriate to believers, being that by which Christ desires to be glorified in us, as Peter also declares, (1 Peter 4:11, 14). But as to ingenuous natures, it is more bitter to suffer disgrace than a hundred deaths, Paul expressly reminds us that not only persecution, but also disgrace awaits us, "because we trust in the living God," (1 Timothy 4:10.) So in another passage he bids us, after his example, walk "by evil report and good report," (2 Corinthians 6:8.)

The cheerfulness required, however, does not imply a total insensibility to pain. The saints could show no patience under the cross if they were not both tortured with pain and grievously molested. Were there no hardship in poverty, no pain in disease, no sting in ignominy, no fear in death, where would be the fortitude and moderation in enduring them?

But while every one of these, by its inherent bitterness, naturally vexes the mind, the believer in this displays his fortitude, that though fully sensible of the bitterness and laboring grievously, he still withstands and struggles boldly; in this displays his patience, that though sharply stung, he is however curbed by the fear of God from breaking forth into any excess; in this displays his alacrity, that though pressed with sorrow and sadness, he rests satisfied with spiritual consolation from God.

Section 9

This conflict which believers maintain against the natural feeling of pain, while they study moderation and patience, Paul elegantly describes in these words: "We are troubled on every side, yet not distressed; we are perplexed, but not in despair; persecuted, but not forsaken; cast down, but not destroyed," (2 Corinthians 4:8, 9.) You see that to bear the cross patiently is not to have your feelings altogether blunted, and to be absolutely insensible to pain, according to the absurd description which the Stoics of old gave of their hero as one who, divested of humanity, was affected in the same way by adversity and prosperity, grief and joy; or rather, like a stone, was not affected by anything.

And what did they gain by that sublime wisdom? they exhibited a shadow of patience, which never did, and never can, exist among men. Nay, rather by aiming at a too exact and rigid patience, they banished it altogether from human life. Now also we have among Christians a new kind of Stoics, who hold it vicious not only to groan and weep, but even to be sad and anxious. These paradoxes are usually started by indolent men who, employing themselves more in speculation than in action, can do nothing else for us than beget such paradoxes.

But we have nothing to do with that iron philosophy which our Lord and Master condemned--not only in word, but also by his own example. For he both grieved and shed tears for his own and others' woes. Nor did he teach his disciples differently: "Ye shall weep and lament, but the world shall rejoice," (John 16:20.) And lest anyone should regard this as vicious, he expressly declares, "Blessed are they that mourn," (Matthew 5:4.) And no wonder. If all tears are condemned, what shall we think of our Lord himself, whose "sweat was as it were great drops of blood falling down to the ground?" (Luke 22:44; Matthew 26:38.) If every kind of fear is a mark of unbelief, what place shall we assign to the dread which, it is said, in no slight degree amazed him; if all sadness is condemned, how shall we justify him when he confesses, "My soul is exceeding sorrowful, even unto death?"

Section 10

I wished to make these observations to keep pious minds from despair, lest, from feeling it impossible to divest themselves of the natural feeling of grief, they might altogether abandon the study of patience. This must necessarily be the result with those who convert patience into stupor, and a brave and firm man into a block. Scripture gives saints the praise of endurance when, though afflicted by the hardships they endure, they are not crushed; though they feel bitterly, they are at the same time filled with spiritual joy; though pressed with anxiety, breathe exhilarated by the consolation of God. Still there is a certain degree of repugnance in their hearts, because natural sense shuns and dreads what is adverse to it, while pious affection, even through these difficulties, tries to obey the divine will.

This repugnance the Lord expressed when he thus addressed Peter: "Verily, verily, I say unto thee, When thou wast young, thou girdedst thyself and walkedst whither thou wouldst; but when thou shalt be old, thou shalt stretch forth thy hands, and another shall gird thee; and carry thee whither thou wouldest not," (John 21:18.) It is not probable, indeed, that when it became necessary to glorify God by death he was driven to it unwilling and resisting; had it been so, little praise would have been due to his martyrdom. But though he obeyed the divine ordination with the greatest alacrity of heart, yet, as he had not divested himself of humanity, he was distracted by a double will. When he thought of the bloody death which he was to die, struck with horror, he would willingly have avoided it: on the other hand, when he considered that it was God who called him to it, his fear was vanquished and suppressed, and he met death cheerfully. It must therefore be our study, if we would be disciples of Christ, to imbue our minds with such reverence and obedience to God as may tame and subjugate all affections contrary to his appointment.

In this way, whatever be the kind of cross to which we are subjected, we shall in the greatest straits firmly maintain our patience. Adversity will have its bitterness, and sting us. When afflicted with disease, we shall groan and be disquieted, and long for health; pressed with poverty, we shall feel the stings of anxiety and sadness, feel the pain of ignominy, contempt, and injury, and pay the tears due to nature at the death of our friends: but our conclusion will always be, The Lord so willed it, therefore let us follow his will. Nay, amid the pungency of grief, among groans and tears this thought will necessarily suggest itself and incline us cheerfully to endure the things for which we are so afflicted.

Section 11

But since the chief reason for enduring the cross has been derived from a consideration of the divine will, we must in few words explain wherein lies the difference between philosophical and Christian patience. Indeed, very few of the philosophers advanced so far as to perceive that the hand of God tries us by means of affliction, and that we ought in this matter to obey God. The only reason which they adduce is, that so it must be. But is not this just to say, that we must yield to God, because it is in vain to contend against him? For if we obey God only because it is necessary, provided we can escape, we shall cease to obey him.

But what Scripture calls us to consider in the will of God is very different, namely, first justice and equity, and then a regard to our own salvation. Hence Christian exhortations to patience are of this nature, Whether poverty, or exile, or imprisonment, or contumely, or disease, or bereavement, or any such evil affects us, we must think that none of them happens except by the will and providence of God; moreover, that everything he does is in the most perfect order. What! Do not our numberless daily faults deserve to be chastised, more severely, and with a heavier rod than his mercy lays upon us? Is it not most right that our flesh should be subdued, and be, as it were, accustomed to the yoke, so as not to rage and wanton as it lists? Are not the justice and the truth of God worthy of our suffering on their account?[9]

But if the equity of God is undoubtedly displayed in affliction, we cannot murmur or struggle against them without iniquity. We no longer hear the frigid cant, Yield, because it is necessary; but a living and energetic precept, Obey, because it is unlawful to resist; bear patiently, because impatience is rebellion against the justice of God. Then as that only seems to us attractive which we perceive to be for our own safety and advantage, here also our heavenly Father consoles us, by the assurance, that in the very cross with which he afflicts us he provides for our salvation. But if it is clear that tribulations are salutary to us, why should we not receive them with calm and grateful minds? In bearing them patiently we are not submitting to necessity but resting satisfied with our own good. The effect of these thoughts is, that to whatever extent our minds are contracted by the bitterness which we naturally feel under the cross, to the same extent will they be expanded with spiritual joy.

Hence arises thanksgiving, which cannot exist unless joy be felt. But if the praise of the Lord and thanksgiving can emanate only from a cheerful and gladdened breasts and there is nothing which ought to interrupt these feelings in us, it is clear how necessary it is to temper the bitterness of the cross with spiritual joy.

---

[9] See end of sec. 4, and sec. 5, 7, 8.

CHAPTER 4

MEDITATING ON THE FUTURE LIFE

Section 1

WHATEVER be the kind of tribulation with which we are afflicted, we should always consider the end of it to be, that we may be trained to despise the present, and thereby stimulated to aspire to the future life. For since God well knows how strongly we are inclined by nature to a slavish love of this world, in order to prevent us from clinging too strongly to it, he employs the fittest reason for calling us back, and shaking off our lethargy. Every one of us, indeed, would be thought to aspire and aim at heavenly immortality during the whole course of his life. For we would be ashamed in no respect to excel the lower animals; whose condition would not be at all inferior to ours, had we not a hope of immortality beyond the grave. But when you attend to the plans, wishes, and actions of each, you see nothing in them but the earth. Hence our stupidity; our minds being dazzled with the glare of wealth, power, and honors, can see no farther.

The heart also, engrossed with avarice, ambition, and lust, is weighed down and cannot rise above them. In short, the whole soul, ensnared by the allurements of the flesh, seeks its happiness on the earth. To meet this disease, the Lord makes his people sensible of the vanity of the present life, by a constant proof of its miseries. Thus, that they may not promise themselves deep and lasting peace in it, he often allows them to be assailed by war, tumult, or rapine, or to be disturbed by other injuries. That they may not long with too much eagerness after fleeting and fading riches, or rest in those which they already possess, he reduces them to want, or, at least, restricts them to a moderate allowance, at one time by exile, at another by sterility, at another by fire, or by other means. That they may not indulge too complacently in the advantages of married life, he either vexes them by the misconduct of their partners, or humbles them by the wickedness of their children, or afflicts them by bereavement.

But if in all these he is indulgent to them, lest they should either swell with vain-glory, or be elated with confidence, by diseases and dangers he sets palpably before them how unstable and evanescent are all the advantages competent to mortals. We duly profit by the discipline of the cross, when we learn that this life, estimated in itself, is restless, troubled, in numberless ways wretched, and plainly in no respect happy; that what are estimated its blessings are uncertain, fleeting, vain, and vitiated by a great admixture of evil. From this we conclude, that all we have to seek or hope for here is contest; that when we think of the crown we must raise our eyes to heaven. For we must hold, that our mind never rises seriously to desire and aspire after the future, until it has learned to despise the present life.

Section 2

For there is no medium between the two things: the earth must either be worthless in our estimation, or keep us enslaved by an intemperate love of it. Therefore, if we have any regard to eternity, we must carefully strive to disencumber ourselves of these fetters. Moreover, since the present life has many enticements to allure us, and great semblance of delight, grace, and sweetness to soothe us, it is of great consequence to us to be now and then called off from its fascinations[10]. For what, pray, would happen, if we here enjoyed an

---

[10] French, "Or pource que la vie presente a tousiours force de delices pour nous attraire, et a grande apparence d'amenité, de grace et de douceur pour nous amieller, il nous est bien mestier d'estre retiré d'heure en d'heure, à ce que nous ne soyons point abusez, et comme ensorcelez de telles flatteries;"--Now because the present life has always a host of delights to attract us, and has great appearance of amenity, grace, and sweetness to entice us, it is of great importance to us to be hourly withdrawn, in order that we may not be deceived, and, as it were, bewitched with such flattery.

uninterrupted course of honor and felicity, when even the constant stimulus of affliction cannot arouse us to a due sense of our misery?

That human life is like smoke or a shadow, is not only known to the learned; there is not a more trite proverb among the vulgar. Considering it a fact most useful to be known, they have recommended it in many well-known expressions. Still there is no fact which we ponder less carefully, or less frequently remember. For we form all our plans just as if we had fixed our immortality on the earth. If we see a funeral, or walk among graves, as the image of death is then present to the eye, I admit we philosophize admirably on the vanity of life. We do not indeed always do so, for those things often have no effect upon us at all. But, at the best, our philosophy is momentary. It vanishes as soon as we turn our back, and leaves not the vestige of remembrance behind; in short, it passes away, just like the applause of a theatre at some pleasant spectacle. Forgetful not only of death, but also of mortality itself, as if no rumor of it had ever reached us, we indulge in supine security as expecting a terrestrial immortality.

Meanwhile, if any one breaks in with the proverb, that man is the creature of a day[11], we indeed acknowledge its truth, but, so far from giving heed to it, the thought of perpetuity still keeps hold of our minds. Who then can deny that it is of the highest importance to us all, I say not, to be admonished by words, but convinced by all possible experience of the miserable condition of our earthly life; since even when convinced we scarcely cease to gaze upon it with vicious, stupid admiration, as if it contained within itself the sum of all that is good? But if God finds it necessary so to train us, it must be our duty to listen to him when he calls, and shakes us from our torpor, that we may hasten to despise the world, and aspire with our whole heart to the future life.

---

[11] Latin, "Animal esse;"--is an ephemereal animal

Section 3

Still the contempt which believers should train themselves to feel for the present life, must not be of a kind to beget hatred of it or ingratitude to God. This life, though abounding in all kinds of wretchedness, is justly classed among divine blessings which are not to be despised. Wherefore, if we do not recognize the kindness of God in it, we are chargeable with no little ingratitude towards him.

To believers, especially, it ought to be a proof of divine benevolence, since it is wholly destined to promote their salvation. Before openly exhibiting the inheritance of eternal glory, God is pleased to manifest himself to us as a Father by minor proofs, viz., the blessings which he daily bestows upon us. Therefore, while this life serves to acquaint us with the goodness of God, shall we disdain it as if it did not contain one particle of good? We ought, therefore, to feel and be affected towards it in such a manner as to place it among those gifts of the divine benignity which are by no means to be despised. Were there no proofs in Scripture, (they are most numerous and clear,) yet nature herself exhorts us to return thanks to God for having brought us forth into light, granted us the use of it, and bestowed upon us all the means necessary for its preservation.

And there is a much higher reason when we reflect that here we are in a manner prepared for the glory of the heavenly kingdom. For the Lord hath ordained, that those who are ultimately to be crowned in heaven must maintain a previous warfare on the earth, that they may not triumph before they have overcome the difficulties of war, and obtained the victory.

Another reason is, that we here begin to experience in various ways a foretaste of the divine benignity, in order that our hope and desire may be whetted for its full manifestation. When once we have concluded that our earthly life is a gift of the divine mercy, of which, agreeably to our obligation, it behooves us to have a grateful remembrance, we shall then properly descend to consider its most wretched condition, and thus escape from that excessive fondness for it, to which, as I have said, we are naturally prone.

Section 4

In proportion as this improper love diminishes, our desire of a better life should increase. I confess, indeed, that a most accurate opinion was formed by those who thought, that the best thing was not to be born, the next best to die early. For, being destitute of the light of God and of true religion, what could they see in it that was not of dire and evil omen? Nor was it unreasonable for those[12] who felt sorrow and shed tears at the birth of their kindred, to keep holiday at their deaths. But this they did without profit; because, devoid of the true doctrine of faith, they saw not how that which in itself is neither happy nor desirable turns to the advantage of the righteous: and hence their opinion issued in despair.

Let believers, then, in forming an estimate of this mortal life, and perceiving that in itself it is nothing but misery, make it their aim to exert themselves with greater alacrity, and less hindrance, in aspiring to the future and eternal life. When we contrast the two, the former may not only be securely neglected, but, in comparison of the latter, be disdained and contemned. If heaven is our country, what can the earth be but a place of exile? If departure from the world is entrance into life, what is the world but a sepulcher, and what is residence in it but immersion in death? If to be freed from the body is to gain full possession of freedom, what is the body but a prison? If it is the very summit of happiness to enjoy the presence of God, is it not miserable to want it? But "whilst we are at home in the body, we are absent from the Lord," (2 Corinthians 5:6.) Thus when the earthly is compared with the heavenly life, it may undoubtedly be despised and trampled underfoot.

We ought never, indeed, to regard it with hatred, except in so far as it keeps us subject to sin; and even this hatred ought not to be directed against life itself. At all events, we must stand so affected towards it in regard to weariness or hatred as, while longing for its

---

[12] French, "Le peuple des Scythes;"--the Scythians.

termination, to be ready at the Lord's will to continue in it, keeping far from everything like murmuring and impatience. For it is as if the Lord had assigned us a post, which we must maintain till he recalls us. Paul, indeed, laments his condition, in being still bound with the fetters of the body, and sighs earnestly for redemption, (Romans 7:24;) nevertheless, he declared that, in obedience to the command of Gods he was prepared for both courses, because he acknowledges it as his duty to God to glorify his name whether by life or by death, while it belongs to God to determine what is most conducive to His glory, (Philippians 1:20-24.) Wherefore, if it becomes us to live and die to the Lord, let us leave the period of our life and death at his disposal. Still let us ardently long for death, and constantly meditate upon it, and in comparison with future immortality, let us despise life, and, on account of the bondage of sin, long to renounce it whenever it shall so please the Lord.

Section 5

But, most strange to say, many who boast of being Christians, instead of thus longing for death, are so afraid of it that they tremble at the very mention of it as a thing ominous and dreadful. We cannot wonder, indeed, that our natural feelings should be somewhat shocked at the mention of our dissolution. But it is altogether intolerable that the light of piety should not be so powerful in a Christian breast as with greater consolation to overcome and suppress that fear. For if we reflect that this our tabernacle, unstable, defective, corruptible, fading, pining, and putrid, is dissolved, in order that it may forthwith be renewed in sure, perfect, incorruptible, in fine, in heavenly glory, will not faith compel us eagerly to desire what nature dreads?

If we reflect that by death we are recalled from exile to inhabit our native country, a heavenly country, shall this give us no comfort? But everything longs for permanent existence. I admit this, and therefore contend that we ought to look to future immortality, where we may obtain that fixed condition which nowhere appears on the earth. For

Paul admirably enjoins believers to hasten cheerfully to death, not because they would be unclothed, but clothed upon," (2 Corinthians 5:2.) Shall the lower animals, and inanimate creatures themselves even wood and stone, as conscious of their present vanity, long for the final resurrection, that they may with the sons of God be delivered from vanity, (Romans 8:19;) and shall we, endued with the light of intellect, and more than intellect, enlightened by the Spirit of God, when our essence is in question, rise no higher than the corruption of this earth? But it is not my purpose, nor is this the place, to plead against this great perverseness.

At the outset, I declared that I had no wish to engage in a diffuse discussion of common-places. My advice to those whose minds are thus timid is to read the short treatise of Cyprian De Mortalitate, unless it be more accordant with their deserts to send them to the philosophers, that by inspecting what they say on the contempt of death, they may begin to blush. This, however let us hold as fixed, that no man has made much progress in the school of Christ who does not look forward with joy to the day of death and final resurrection, (2 Timothy 4:18; Titus 2:13:) for Paul distinguishes all believers by this mark; and the usual course of Scripture is to direct us thither whenever it would furnish us with an argument for substantial joy. "Look up," says our Lord, "and lift up your heads: for your redemption draweth nigh," (Luke 21:28.) Is it reasonable, I ask, that what he intended to have a powerful effect in stirring us up to alacrity and exultation should produce nothing but sadness and consternation? If it is so, why do we still glory in him as our Master?

Therefore, let us come to a sounder mind, and how repugnant so ever the blind and stupid longing of the flesh may be, let us doubt not to desire the advent of the Lord not in wish only, but with earnest sighs, as the most propitious of all events. He will come as a Redeemer to deliver us from an immense abyss of evil and misery, and lead us to the blessed inheritance of his life and glory.

Section 6

Thus, indeed, it is; the whole body of the faithful, so long as they live on the earth, must be like sheep for the slaughter, in order that they may be conformed to Christ their head, (Romans 8:36.) Most deplorable, therefore, would their situation be did they not, by raising their mind to heaven, become superior to all that is in the world, and rise above the present aspect of affairs, (1 Corinthians 15:19.)

On the other hand, when once they have raised their head above all earthly objects, though they see the wicked flourishing in wealth and honor, and enjoying profound peace, indulging in luxury and splendor, and reveling in all kinds of delights, though they should moreover be wickedly assailed by them, suffer insult from their pride, be robbed by their avarice, or assailed by any other passion, they will have no difficulty in bearing up under these evils. They will turn their eye to that day, (Isaiah 25:8; Revelation 7:17,) on which the Lord will receive his faithful servants, wipe away all tears from their eyes, clothe them in a robe of glory and joy, feed them with the ineffable sweetness of his pleasures, exalt them to share with him in his greatness; in fine, admit them to a participation in his happiness.

But the wicked who may have flourished on the earth, he will cast forth in extreme ignominy, will change their delights into torments, their laughter and joy into wailing and gnashing of teeth, their peace into the gnawing of conscience, and punish their luxury with unquenchable fire. He will also place their necks under the feet of the godly, whose patience they abused. For, as Paul declares, "it is a righteous thing with God to recompense tribulation to them that trouble you; and to you who are troubled rest with us, when the Lord Jesus shall be revealed from heaven," (2 Thessalonians 1:6, 7.)

This, indeed, is our only consolation; deprived of it, we must either give way to despondency, or resort to our destruction to the vain solace of the world. The Psalmist confesses, "My feet were almost gone: my steps had well nigh slipt: for I was envious at the foolish when I saw the prosperity of the wicked," (Psalm 73:3, 4) and he found no resting-place until he entered the sanctuary, and considered the latter end of the righteous and the wicked. To conclude in one word, the cross of Christ then only triumphs in the breasts of believers over the devil and the flesh, sin and sinners, when their eyes are directed to the power of his resurrection.

CHAPTER 5

HOW TO DEAL WITH THE PRESENT LIFE
AND ITS COMFORTS

Section 1

BY such rudiments we are at the same time well instructed by Scripture in the proper use of earthly blessings, a subject which, in forming a scheme of life, is by no mean to be neglected. For if we are to live, we must use the necessary supports of life; nor can we even shun those things which seem more subservient to delight than to necessity. We must therefore observe a mean, that we may use them with a pure conscience, whether for necessity or for pleasure. This the Lord prescribes by his word, when he tells us that to his people the present life is a kind of pilgrimage by which they hasten to the heavenly kingdom. If we are only to pass through the earth, there can be no doubt that we are to use its blessings only in so far as they assist our progress, rather than retard it.

Accordingly, Paul, not without cause, admonishes us to use this world without abusing it, and to buy possessions as if we were selling them (1 Corinthians 7:30, 31). But as this is a slippery place, and there is great danger of falling on either side, let us fix our feet where we can stand safely. There have been some good and holy men who, when they saw intemperance and luxury perpetually carried to excess, if not strictly curbed, and were desirous to correct so pernicious an evil, imagined that there was no other method than to allow man to use corporeal goods only in so far as they were necessaries: a counsel pious indeed, but unnecessarily austere; for it does the very dangerous thing of binding consciences in closer fetters than those in which they are bound by the word of God.

Moreover, necessity, according to them[13], was abstinence from everything which could be wanted, so that they held it scarcely lawful to make any addition to bread and water. Others were still more austere, as is related of Cratetes the Theban, who threw his riches into the sea, because he thought, that unless he destroyed them they would destroy him. Many also in the present day, while they seek a pretext for carnal intemperance in the use of external things, and at the same time would pave the way for licentiousness, assume for granted, what I by no means concede, that this liberty is not to be restrained by any modification, but that it is to be left to every man's conscience to use them as far as he thinks lawful. I indeed confess that here consciences neither can nor ought to be bound by fixed and definite laws; but that Scripture having laid down general rules for the legitimate uses we should keep within the limits which they prescribe.

Section 2

Let this be our principle, that we err not in the use of the gifts of Providence when we refer them to the end for which their author made and destined them, since he created them for our good, and not for our destruction. No man will keep the true path better than he who shall have this end carefully in view. Now then, if we consider for what end he created food, we shall find that he consulted not only for our necessity, but also for our enjoyment and delight. Thus, in clothing, the end was, in addition to necessity, comeliness and honor; and in herbs, fruits, and trees, besides their various uses, gracefulness of appearance and sweetness of smell. Were it not so, the Prophet would not enumerate among the mercies of God "wine that maketh glad the heart of man, and oil to make his face to shine," (Psalm 104:15.)

---

[13] See Chrysost. ad Heb. Hi. As to Cratetes the Theban, see Plutarch, Lib. de Vitand. aere alien. and Philostratus in Vita Apollonii.

The Scriptures would not everywhere mention, in commendation of his benignity, that he had given such things to men. The natural qualities of things themselves demonstrate to what end, and how far, they may be lawfully enjoyed. Has the Lord adorned flowers with all the beauty which spontaneously presents itself to the eye, and the sweet odor which delights the sense of smell, and shall it be unlawful for us to enjoy that beauty and this odor? What? Has he not so distinguished colors as to make some more agreeable than others? Has he not given qualities to gold and silver, ivory and marble, thereby rendering them precious above other metals or stones? In short, has he not given many things a value without having any necessary use?

Section 3

Have done, then, with that inhuman philosophy which, in allowing no use of the creatures but for necessity, not only maliciously deprives us of the lawful fruit of the divine beneficence, but cannot be realized without depriving man of all his senses, and reducing him to a block. But, on the other hand, let us with no less care guard against the lusts of the flesh, which, if not kept in order, break through all bounds, and are, as I have said, advocated by those who, under pretence of liberty, allow themselves every sort of license.

First one restraint is imposed when we hold that the object of creating all things was to teach us to know their author, and feel grateful for his indulgence. Where is the gratitude if you so gorge or stupefy yourself with feasting and wine as to be unfit for offices of piety, or the duties of your calling? Where the recognition of God, if the flesh, boiling forth in lust through excessive indulgences infects the mind with its impurity, so as to lose the discernment of' honor and rectitude? Where thankfulness to God for clothing, if on account of sumptuous raiment we both admire ourselves and disdain others? if, from a love of show and splendor, we pave the way for immodesty? Where our recognition of God, if the glare of these things captivates our minds? For many are so devoted to luxury in all their senses that their mind lies buried: many are so delighted with marble, gold, and pictures, that they become marble-hearted--are changed as it were into metal, and made like painted figures. The kitchen, with its savory smells, so engrosses them that they have no spiritual savor. The same thing may be seen in other matters.

Wherefore, it is plain that there is here great necessity for curbing licentious abuse, and conforming to the rule of Paul, "make not provision for the flesh to fulfill the lusts thereof," (Romans 13:14.) Where too much liberty is given to them, they break forth without measure or restraint.

Section 4

There is no surer or quicker way of accomplishing this than by despising the present life and aspiring to celestial immortality. For hence two rules arise: First, "it remaineth, that both they that have wives be as though they had none;" "and they that use this world, as not abusing it," (1 Corinthains 7:29, 31.) Secondly, we must learn to be no less placid and patient in enduring penury, than moderate in enjoying abundance.

He who makes it his rule to use this world as if he used it not, not only cuts off all gluttony in regard to meat and drink, and all effeminacy, ambition, pride, excessive shows and austerity, in regard to his table, his house, and his clothes, but removes every care and affection which might withdraw or hinder him from aspiring to the heavenly life, and cultivating the interest of his soul[14]. It was well said by Cato: Luxury causes great care, and produces great carelessness as to virtue; and it is an old proverb,--Those who are much occupied with the care of the body, usually give little care to the soul.

---

[14] French, "Parer notre ame de ses vrais ornemens;"--deck our soul with its true ornaments.

Therefore while the liberty of the Christian in external matters is not to be tied down to a strict rule, it is, however, subject to this law--he must indulge as little as possible; on the other hand, it must be his constant aims not only to curb luxury, but to cut off all show of superfluous abundance, and carefully beware of converting a help into an hindrance.

Section 5

Another rule is, that those in narrow and slender circumstances should learn to bear their wants patiently, that they may not become immoderately desirous of things, the moderate use of which implies no small progress in the school of Christ. For in addition to the many other vices which accompany a longing for earthly good, he who is impatient under poverty almost always betrays the contrary disease in abundance.

By this I mean, that he who is ashamed of a sordid garment will be vain-glorious of a splendid one; he who not contented with a slender, feels annoyed at the want of a more luxurious supper, will intemperately abuse his luxury if he obtains it; he who has a difficulty, and is dissatisfied in submitting to a private and humble condition, will be unable to refrain from pride if he attain to honor. Let it be the aim of all who have any unfeigned desire for piety to learn, after the example of the Apostle, "both to be full and to be hungry, both to abound and to suffer need," (Philippians 4:12.) Scripture, moreover, has a third rule for modifying the use of earthly blessings. We have already adverted to it when considering the offices of charity. For it declares that they have all been given us by the kindness of God, and appointed for our use under the condition of being regarded as trusts, of which we must one day give account. We must, therefore, administer them as if we constantly heard the words sounding in our ears, "Give an account of your stewardship."

At the same time, let us remember by whom the account is to be taken, viz., by him who, while he so highly commends abstinence, sobriety, frugality, and moderation, abominates luxury, pride, ostentation, and vanity; who approves of no administration but that which is combined with charity, who with his own lips has already condemned all those pleasures which withdraw the heart from chastity and purity, or darken the intellect.

Section 6

The last thing to be observed is, that the Lord enjoins every one of us, in all the actions of life, to have respect to our own calling. He knows the boiling restlessness of the human mind, the fickleness with which it is borne hither and thither, its eagerness to hold opposites at one time in its grasp, its ambition. Therefore, lest all things should be thrown into confusion by our folly and rashness, he has assigned distinct duties to each in the different modes of life. And that no one may presume to overstep his proper limits, he has distinguished the different modes of life by the name of callings. Every man's mode of life, therefore, is a kind of station assigned him by the Lord, that he may not be always driven about at random. So necessary is this distinction, that all our actions are thereby estimated in his sight, and often in a very different way from that in which human reason or philosophy would estimate them. There is no more illustrious deed even among philosophers than to free one's country from tyranny, and yet the private individual who stabs the tyrant is openly condemned by the voice of the heavenly Judge.

But I am unwilling to dwell on particular examples; it is enough to know that in everything the call of the Lord is the foundation and beginning of right action. He who does not act with reference to it will never, in the discharge of duty, keep the right path. He will sometimes be able, perhaps, to give the semblance of something laudable, but whatever it may be in the sight of man, it will be rejected before the throne of God; and besides, there will be no harmony in the different parts of his life. Hence, he only who directs his life to this end will have it properly framed; because free from the impulse of rashness, he will not attempt more than his calling justifies, knowing that it is unlawful to overleap the prescribed bounds. He who is obscure will not decline to cultivate a private life, that he may not desert the post at which God has placed him.

Again, in all our cares, toils, annoyances, and other burdens, it will be no small alleviation to know that all these are under the superintendence of God. The magistrate will more willingly perform his office, and the father of a family confine himself to his proper sphere. Everyone in his particular mode of life will, without repining, suffer its inconveniences, cares, uneasiness, and anxiety, persuaded that God has laid on the burden. This, too, will afford admirable consolation, that in following your proper calling, no work will be so mean and sordid as not to have a splendor and value in the eye of God

OF PRAYER

A PERPETUAL EXERCISE OF FAITH
THE DAILY BENEFITS DERIVED FROM IT

CHAPTER 1

- *A general summary of what is contained
  in the previous part of the work.*

- *A transition to the doctrine of prayer.*

- *Prayer's connection with the subject of faith.*

FROM the previous part of the work we clearly see how completely destitute man is of all good, how devoid of every means of procuring his own salvation. Hence, if he would obtain succor in his necessity, he must go beyond himself, and procure it in some other quarter. It has farther been shown that the Lord kindly and spontaneously manifests himself in Christ, in whom he offers all happiness for our misery, all abundance for our want, opening up the treasures of heaven to us, so that we may turn with full faith to his beloved Son, depend upon him with full expectation, rest in him, and cleave to him with full hope. This, indeed, is that secret and hidden philosophy which cannot be learned by syllogisms: a philosophy thoroughly understood by those whose eyes God has so opened as to see light in his light (Psalm 36:9).

But after we have learned by faith to know that whatever is necessary for us or defective in us is supplied in God and in our Lord Jesus Christ, in whom it hath pleased the Father that all fullness should dwell, that we may thence draw as from an inexhaustible fountain, it remains for us to seek and in prayer implore of him what we have learned to be in him. To know God as the sovereign disposer of all good, inviting us to present our requests, and yet not to approach or ask of him, were so far from availing us, that it were just as if one told of a treasure were to allow it to remain buried in the ground.

Hence the Apostle, to show that a faith unaccompanied with prayer to God cannot be genuine, states this to be the order: As faith springs from the Gospel, so by faith our hearts are framed to call upon the name of God (Romans 10:14). And this is the very thing which he had expressed some time before, viz., that the Spirit of adoption, which seals the testimony of the Gospel on our hearts, gives us courage to make our requests known unto God, calls forth groanings which cannot be uttered, and enables us to cry, Abba, Father (Romans 8:26). This last point, as we have hitherto only touched upon it slightly in passing, must now be treated more fully.

CHAPTER 2

- *The definition of prayer.*

- *The necessity and use of prayer.*

To prayer, then, are we indebted for penetrating to those riches which are treasured up for us with our heavenly Father? For there is a kind of intercourse between God and men, by which, having entered the upper sanctuary, they appear before Him and appeal to his promises, that when necessity requires they may learn by experiences that what they believed merely on the authority of his word was not in vain. Accordingly, we see that nothing is set before us as an object of expectation from the Lord which we are not enjoined to ask of Him in prayer, so true it is that prayer digs up those treasures which the Gospel of our Lord discovers to the eye of faith.

The necessity and utility of this exercise of prayer no words can sufficiently express. Assuredly it is not without cause our heavenly Father declares that our only safety is in calling upon his name, since by it we invoke the presence of his providence to watch over our interests, of his power to sustain us when weak and almost fainting, of his goodness to receive us into favor, though miserably loaded with sin; in fine, call upon him to manifest himself to us in all his perfections. Hence, admirable peace and tranquility are given to our consciences; for the straits by which we were pressed being laid before the Lord, we rest fully satisfied with the assurance that none of our evils are unknown to him, and that he is both able and willing to make the best provision for us.

CHAPTER 3

- *Isn't prayer useless, because God already knows our wants?
  A response from the institution and end of prayer and
  a confirmation by example.*

- *Prayer's necessity and propriety.*

- *Prayer perpetually reminds us of our duty, and leads us to
  meditation on divine providence.*

- *Prayer is a most useful exercise as proved by
  three passages of Scripture.*

But someone will say, Does he not know without a monitor both what our difficulties are, and what is meet for our interest, so that it seems in some measure superfluous to solicit him by our prayers, as if he were winking, or even sleeping, until aroused by the sound of our voice[1]? Those who argue thus attend not to the end for which the Lord taught us to pray. It was not so much for his sake as for ours. He wills indeed, as is just, that due honor be paid him by acknowledging that all which men desire or feel to be useful, and pray to obtain, is derived from him. But even the benefit of the homage which we thus pay him redounds to ourselves. Hence the holy patriarchs, the more confidently they proclaimed the mercies of God to themselves and others felt the stronger incitement to prayer. It will be sufficient to refer to the example of Elijah, who being assured of the purpose of God had good ground for the promise of rain which he gives to Ahab, and yet prays anxiously upon his knees, and sends his servant seven

---

[1] French, "Dont il sembleroit que ce fust chose supeflue de le soliciter par prieres; veu que nous avons accoustumé de soliciter ceux qui ne pensent à nostre affaire, et qui sont endormis."--Whence it would seem that it was a superfluous matter to solicit him by prayer; seeing we are accustomed to solicit those who think not of our business and who are slumbering.

times to inquire (1 Kings 18:42); not that he discredits the oracle, but because he knows it to be his duty to lay his desires before God, lest his faith should become drowsy or torpid.

Wherefore, although it is true that while we are listless or insensible to our wretchedness, he wakes and watches for us and sometimes even assists us unasked; it is very much for our interest to be constantly supplicating him; first, that our heart may always be inflamed with a serious and ardent desire of seeking, loving and serving him, while we accustom ourselves to have recourse to him as a sacred anchor in every necessity; secondly, that no desires, no longing whatever, of which we are ashamed to make him the witness, may enter our minds, while we learn to place all our wishes in his sight, and thus pour out our heart before him; and, lastly, that we may be prepared to receive all his benefits with true gratitude and thanksgiving, while our prayers remind us that they proceed from his hand. Moreover, having obtained what we asked, being persuaded that he has answered our prayers, we are led to long more earnestly for his favor, and at the same time have greater pleasure in welcoming the blessings which we perceive to have been obtained by our prayers.

Lastly, use and experience confirm the thought of his providence in our minds in a manner adapted to our weakness, when we understand that he not only promises that he will never fail us, and spontaneously gives us access to approach him in every time of need, but has his hand always stretched out to assist his people, not amusing them with words, but proving himself to be a present aid. For these reasons, though our most merciful Father never slumbers nor sleeps, he very often seems to do so, that thus he may exercise us, when we might otherwise be listless and slothful, in asking, entreating, and earnestly beseeching him to our great good.

It is very absurd, therefore, to dissuade men from prayer, by pretending that Divine Providence, which is always watching over the government of the universes is in vain importuned by our supplications, when, on the contrary, the Lord himself declares, that he is "nigh unto all that call upon him, to all that call upon him in truth (Psalm 145:18). No better is the frivolous allegation of others, that it is superfluous to pray for things which the Lord is ready of his own accord to bestow; since it is his pleasure that those very things which flow from his spontaneous liberality should be acknowledged as conceded to our prayers. This is testified by that memorable sentence in the psalms to which many others corresponds: "The eyes of the Lord are upon the righteous, and his ears are open unto their cry" (Psalm 34:15). This passage, while extolling the care which Divine Providence spontaneously exercises over the safety of believers, omits not the exercise of faith by which the mind is aroused from sloth. The eyes of God are awake to assist the blind in their necessity, but he is likewise pleased to listen to our groans, that he may give us the better proof of his love. And thus both things are true, "He that keepeth Israel shall neither slumber nor sleep" (Psalm 121:4); and yet whenever he sees us dumb and torpid, he withdraws as if he had forgotten us.

CHAPTER 4.

- *The first rule of prayer: Reverence toward God,*
  or how the mind ought to be composed.

Let the first rule of right prayer then be, to have our heart and mind framed as becomes those who are entering into converse with God. This we shall accomplish in regard to the mind, if, laying aside carnal thoughts and cares which might interfere with the direct and pure contemplation of God, it not only be wholly intent on prayer, but also, as far as possible, be borne and raised above itself. I do not here insist on a mind so disengaged as to feel none of the gnawings of anxiety; on the contrary, it is by much anxiety that the fervor of prayer is inflamed. Thus we see that the holy servants of God betray great anguish, not to say solicitude, when they cause the voice of complaint to ascend to the Lord from the deep abyss and the jaws of death. What I say is, that all foreign and extraneous cares must be dispelled by which the mind might be driven to and fro in vague suspense, be drawn down from heaven, and kept groveling on the earth. When I say it must be raised above itself, I mean that it must not bring into the presence of God any of those things which our blind and stupid reason is wont to devise, nor keep itself confined within the little measure of its own vanity, but rise to a purity worthy of God.

CHAPTER 5

- *Giddiness must be excluded, and all our feelings seriously engaged, shown by lifting the hand in prayer.*

- *We must ask only what God permits.*

- *To help our weakness, God gives the Spirit to be our guide in prayer.*

- *The office of the Spirit.*

- *We must pray both with the heart and the lips.*

Both things are especially worthy of notice. First, let everyone in professing to pray turn thither all his thoughts and feelings, and be not (as is usual) distracted by wandering thoughts; because nothing is more contrary to the reverence due to God than that levity which bespeaks a mind too much given to license and devoid of fear. In this matter we ought to labor the more earnestly the more difficult we experience it to be; for no man is so intent on prayer as not to feel many thoughts creeping in, and either breaking off the tenor of his prayer, or retarding it by some turning or digression. Here let us consider how unbecoming it is when God admits us to familiar intercourse to abuse his great condescension by mingling things sacred and profane, reverence for him not keeping our minds under restraint; but just as if in prayer we were conversing with one like ourselves forgetting him, and allowing our thoughts to run to and fro.

Let us know, then, that none duly prepare themselves for prayer but those who are so impressed with the majesty of God that they engage in it free from all earthly cares and affections. The ceremony of lifting up our hands in prayer is designed to remind us that we are far removed from God, unless our thoughts rise upward: as it is said in the psalm, "Unto thee, O Lord, do I lift up my soul" (Psalm 25:1). And Scripture repeatedly uses the expression to raise our prayers meaning that those who would be heard by God must not grovel in the mire. The sum is, that the more liberally God deals with us, condescendingly inviting us to disburden our cares into his bosom, the less excusable we are if this admirable and incomparable blessing does not in our estimation outweigh all other things, and win our affection, that prayer may seriously engage our every thought and feeling. This cannot be unless our mind, strenuously exerting itself against all impediments, rise upward.

Our second proposition was, that we are to ask only in so far as God permits. For though he bids us pour out our hearts (Psalm 62:8), he does not indiscriminately give loose reins to foolish and depraved affections; and when he promises that he will grant believers their wish, his indulgence does not proceed so far as to submit to their caprice. In both matters grievous delinquencies are everywhere committed. For not only do many without modesty, without reverence, presume to invoke God concerning their frivolities, but impudently bring forward their dreams, whatever they may be, before the tribunal of God. Such is the folly or stupidity under which they labor, that they have the hardihood to obtrude upon God desires so vile, that they would blush exceedingly to impart them to their fellow men. Profane writers have derided and even expressed their detestation of this presumption, and yet the vice has always prevailed. Hence, as the ambitious adopted Jupiter as their patron; the avaricious, Mercury; the literary aspirants, Apollo and Minerva; the warlike, Mars; the licentious, Venus: so in the present day, as I lately observed, men in prayer give greater license to their unlawful desires than if they were telling jocular tales among their equals. God does not suffer his condescension to be thus mocked, but vindicating his own light, places our wishes under the restraint of his authority. We must, therefore, attend to the observation of John: "This is the confidence that we have in him, that if we ask anything according to his will, he heareth us" (1 John 5:14). But as our faculties are far from being able to attain to such high perfection, we must seek for some means to assist them. As the eye of our mind should be intent upon God, so the affection of our heart ought to follow in the same course. But both fall far beneath this, or rather, they faint and fail, and are carried in a contrary direction. To assist this weakness, God gives us the guidance of the Spirit in our prayers to dictate what is right, and regulate our affections. For seeing "we know not what we should pray for as we ought," "the Spirit itself maketh intercession for us with groanings which cannot be uttered" (Romans 8:26) not that he actually prays or groans, but he excites in us sighs, and wishes, and confidence, which our natural powers are not at all able to conceive. Nor is it without cause Paul gives the name of groanings which cannot be uttered to the prayers which believers send forth under the guidance of the Spirit. For those who are truly exercised in prayer are not unaware that blind anxieties so restrain and perplex them, that they can scarcely find what it becomes them to utter; nay, in attempting to lisp they halt and hesitate. Hence it appears that to pray aright is a special gift. We do not speak thus in indulgence to our sloths as if we were to leave the office of prayer to the Holy Spirit, and give way to that carelessness to which we are too prone. Thus we sometimes hear the impious expression, that we are to wait in suspense until he take possession of our minds while otherwise occupied.

Our meaning is, that, weary of our own heartlessness and sloth, we are to long for the aid of the Spirit. Nor, indeed, does Paul, when he enjoins us to pray in the Spirit (1 Corinthians 14:15), cease to exhort us to vigilance, intimating, that while the inspiration of the Spirit is effectual to the formation of prayer, it by no means impedes or retards our own endeavors; since in this matter God is pleased to try how efficiently faith influences our hearts.

CHAPTER 6

- *The second rule of prayer, we need a sense of our true want.*

- *This second rule can be violated:*

    a. By perfunctory and formal prayer

    b. By hypocrites who have no sense of their sins.

    c. By giddiness in prayer.

Another rule of prayer is, that in asking we must always truly feel our wants, and seriously considering that we need all the things which we ask, accompany the prayer with a sincere, nay, ardent desire of obtaining them. Many repeat prayers in a perfunctory manner from a set form, as if they were performing a task to God, and though they confess that this is a necessary remedy for the evils of their condition, because it were fatal to be left without the divine aid which they implore, it still appears that they perform the duty from custom, because their minds are meanwhile cold, and they ponder not what they ask. A general and confused feeling of their necessity leads them to pray, but it does not make them solicitous as in a matter of present consequence, that they may obtain the supply of their need.

Moreover, can we suppose anything more hateful or even more execrable to God than this fiction of asking the pardon of sins, while he who asks at the very time either thinks that he is not a sinner, or, at least, is not thinking that he is a sinner; in other words, a fiction by which God is plainly held in derision? But mankind, as I have lately said, are full of depravity, so that in the way of perfunctory service they often ask many things of God which they think come to them without his beneficence, or from some other quarter, or are already certainly in their possession. There is another fault which seems less heinous, but is not to be tolerated. Some murmur out prayers without meditation, their only principle being that God is to be propitiated by prayer. Believers ought to be especially on their guard never to appear in the presence of God with the intention of presenting a request unless they are under some serious impression, and are, at the same time, desirous to obtain it. Nay, although in these things which we ask only for the glory of God, we seem not at first sight to consult for our necessity, yet we ought not to ask with less fervor and vehement desire. For instance, when we pray that his name be hallowed -- that hallowing must, so to speak, be earnestly hungered and thirsted after.

CHAPTER 7

- *We must pray always.*

- *This is confirmed by an examination of the dangers by which both our life and our salvation are constantly threatened.*

- *Confirmed further by the command of God, by the nature of true repentance, and a consideration of impenitence.*

If it is objected, that the necessity which urges us to pray is not always equal, I admit it, and this distinction is profitably taught us by James: "Is any among you afflicted? Let him pray. Is any merry? Let him sing psalms" (James 5:13). Therefore, common sense itself dictates, that as we are too sluggish, we must be stimulated by God to pray earnestly whenever the occasion requires. This David calls a time when God "may be found" (a seasonable time); because, as he declares in several other passages, that the more hardly grievances, annoyances, fears, and other kinds of trial press us, the freer is our access to God, as if he were inviting us to himself. Still not less true is the injunction of Paul to pray "always" (Ephesians 6:18); because, however prosperously according to our view, things proceed, and however we may be surrounded on all sides with grounds of joy, there is not an instant of time during which our want does not exhort us to prayer. A man abounds in wheat and wine; but as he cannot enjoy a morsel of bread, unless by the continual bounty of God, his granaries or cellars will not prevent him from asking for daily bread. Then, if we consider how many dangers impend every moment, fear itself will teach us that no time ought to be without prayer. This, however, may be better known in spiritual matters. For when will the many sins of which we are conscious allow us to sit secure without suppliantly entreating freedom from guilt and punishment? When will temptation give us a truce, making it unnecessary to hasten for help?

Moreover, zeal for the kingdom and glory of God ought not to seize us by starts, but urge us without intermission, so that every time should appear seasonable. It is not without cause, therefore, that assiduity in prayer is so often enjoined. I am not now speaking of perseverance, which shall afterwards be considered; but Scripture, by reminding us of the necessity of constant prayer, charges us with sloth, because we feel not how much we stand in need of this care and assiduity. By this rule hypocrisy and the device of lying to God are restrained, nay, altogether banished from prayer. God promises that he will be near to those who call upon him in truth, and declares that those who seek him with their whole heart will find him: those, therefore, who delight in their own pollution, cannot surely aspire to him.

One of the requisites of legitimate prayer is repentance. Hence the common declaration of Scripture, that God does not listen to the wicked; that their prayers, as well as their sacrifices, are an abomination to him. For it is right that those who seal up their hearts should find the ears of God closed against them, that those who, by their hardheartedness, provoke his severity should find him inflexible. In Isaiah he thus threatens: "When ye make many prayers, I will not hear: your hands are full of blood" (Isaiah 1:15). In like manner, in Jeremiah, "Though they shall cry unto me, I will not hearken unto them" (Jeremiah 11:7, 8, 11); because he regards it as the highest insult for the wicked to boast of his covenant while profaning his sacred name by their whole lives. Hence he complains in Isaiah: "This people draw near to me with their mouth, and with their lips do honor me; but have removed their heart far from men" (Isaiah 29:13). Indeed, he does not confine this to prayers alone, but declares that he abominates pretense in every part of his service. Hence the words of James, "Ye ask and receive not, because ye ask amiss, that ye may consume it upon your lusts" (James 4:3). It is true, indeed (as we shall again see in a little), that the pious, in the prayers which they utter, trust not to their own worth; still the admonition of John is not superfluous: "Whatsoever we ask, we receive of him, because we keep his commandments" (1 John 3:22); an evil conscience shuts the door against us.

Hence it follows, that none but the sincere worshippers of God pray aright, or are listened to. Let everyone, therefore, who prepares to pray feel dissatisfied with what is wrong in his condition, and assume, which he cannot do without repentance, the character and feelings of a poor suppliant.

CHAPTER 8

• The third rule of prayer: suppressing all pride.
Examples: Daniel, David, Isaiah, Jeremiah, Baruch.

The third rule to be added is: that he who comes into the presence of God to pray must divest himself of all vainglorious thoughts, lay aside all idea of worth; in short, discard all self-confidence, humbly giving God the whole glory, lest by arrogating anything, however little, to himself, vain pride cause him to turn away his face. Of this submission, which casts down all haughtiness, we have numerous examples in the servants of God. The holier they are, the more humbly they prostrate themselves when they come into the presence of the Lord.

Thus Daniel, on whom the Lord himself bestowed such high commendation, says, "We do not present our supplications before thee for our righteousness but for thy great mercies. O Lord, hear; O Lord, forgive; O Lord, hearken and do; defer not, for thine own sake, O my God: for thy city and thy people are called by thy name." This he does not indirectly in the usual manner, as if he were one of the individuals in a crowd: he rather confesses his guilt apart, and as a suppliant betaking himself to the asylum of pardon, he distinctly declares that he was confessing his own sin, and the sin of his people Israel (Daniel 9:18-20).

David also sets us an example of this humility: "Enter not into judgment with thy servant: for in thy sight shall no man living be justified" (Psalm 143:2).

In like manner, Isaiah prays, "Behold, thou art wroth; for we have sinned: in those is continuance, and we shall be saved. But we are all as an unclean thing, and all our righteousnesses are as filthy rags; and we all do fade as a leaf; and our iniquities, like the wind, have taken us away. And there is none that calleth upon thy name, that stirreth up himself to take hold of thee: for thou hast hid thy face from us, and hast consumed us, because of our iniquities. But now, O Lord, thou art our Father; we are the clay, and thou our potter; and we all are the work of thy hand. Be not wroth very sore, O Lord, neither remember iniquity for ever: Behold, see, we beseech thee, we are all thy people." (Isaiah 64:5-9). You see how they put no confidence in anything but this: considering that they are the Lord's, they despair not of being the objects of his care.

In the same way, Jeremiah says, "O Lord, though our iniquities testify against us, do thou it for thy name's sake" (Jeremiah 14:7).

For it was most truly and piously written by the uncertain author (whoever he may have been) that wrote the book which is attributed to the prophet Baruch[2], "But the soul that is greatly vexed, which goeth stooping and feeble, and the eyes that fail, and the hungry soul, will give thee praise and righteousness, O Lord. Therefore, we do not make our humble supplication before thee, O Lord our God, for the righteousness of our fathers, and of our kings." "Hear, O Lord, and have mercy; for thou art merciful: and have pity upon us, because we have sinned before thee" (Baruch 2:18, 19; 3:2).

---

[2] French, "Pourtant ce qui est escrit en la prophetie qu'on attribue à Baruch, combien que l'autheur soit incertain, est tres sainctement dit;"--However, what is written in the prophecy which is attributed to Baruch, though the author is uncertain, is very holily said.

CHAPTER 9

- *The primary advantage of thus suppressing pride: it leads to earnest entreaty for pardon, accompanied with humble confession and sure confidence in the Divine mercy.*

- *A general introduction to procure favor to our prayers should never be omitted.*

In fine, supplication for pardon, with humble and ingenuous confession of guilt, forms both the preparation and commencement of right prayer. For the holiest of men cannot hope to obtain anything from God until he has been freely reconciled to him. God cannot be propitious to any but those whom he pardons. Hence it is not strange that this is the key by which believers open the door of prayer, as we learn from several passages in The Psalms. David, when presenting a request on a different subject, says, "Remember not the sins of my youth, nor my transgressions; according to thy mercy remember me, for thy goodness sake, O Lord" (Psalm 25:7). Again, "Look upon my affliction and my pain, and forgive my sins" (Psalm 25:18). Here also we see that it is not sufficient to call ourselves to account for the sins of each passing day; we must also call to mind those which might seem to have been long before buried in oblivion. For in another passage the same prophet, confessing one grievous crime, takes occasion to go back to his very birth, "I was shapen in iniquity, and in sin did my mother conceive me" (Psalm 51:5); not to extenuate the fault by the corruption of his nature, but as it were to accumulate the sins of his whole life, that the stricter he was in condemning himself, the more placable God might be.

But although the saints do not always in express terms ask forgiveness of sins, yet if we carefully ponder those prayers as given in Scripture, the truth of what I say will readily appear; namely, that their courage to pray was derived solely from the mercy of God, and that they always began with appeasing him. For when a man interrogates his conscience, so far is he from presuming to lay his cares familiarly before God, that if he did not trust to mercy and pardon, he would tremble at the very thought of approaching him. There is, indeed, another special confession. When believers long for deliverance from punishment, they at the same time pray that their sins may be pardoned[3]; for it were absurd to wish that the effect should be taken away while the cause remains. For we must beware of imitating foolish patients who, anxious only about curing accidental symptoms, neglect the root of the disease[4]. Nay, our endeavor must be to have God propitious even before he attests his favor by external signs, both because this is the order which he himself chooses, and it were of little avail to experience his kindness, did not conscience feel that he is appeased, and thus enable us to regard him as altogether lovely. Of this we are even reminded by our Savior's reply. Having determined to cure the paralytic, he says, "Thy sins are forgiven thee;" in other words, he raises our thoughts to the object which is especially to be desired, viz. admission into the favor of God, and then gives the fruit of reconciliation by bringing assistance to us.

But besides that special confession of present guilt which believers employ, in supplicating for pardon of every fault and punishment, that general introduction which procures favor for our prayers must never be omitted, because prayers will never reach God unless they are founded on free mercy. To this we may refer the words of John, "If we confess our sins, he is faithful and just to forgive us our sins and to cleanse us from all unrighteousness" (1 John 1:9).

---

[3] French, "il reconoissent le chastisement qu'ils ont merité;"--they acknowledge the punishment which they have deserved.

[4] The French adds, "Ils voudront qu'on leur oste le mal de tests et des reins, et seront contens qu'on ne touche point a la fievre;"--They would wish to get quit of the pain in the head and the loins, and would be contented to leave the fever untouched.

Hence, under the law it was necessary to consecrate prayers by the expiation of blood, both that they might be accepted, and that the people might be warned that they were unworthy of the high privilege until, being purged from their defilements, they founded their confidence in prayer entirely on the mercy of God.

CHAPTER 10

• A common objection to the third rule of prayer answered.

Sometimes, however, the saints in supplicating God, seem to appeal to their own righteousness, as when David says, "Preserve my soul; for I am holy" (Psalm 86:2). Also Hezekiah, "Remember now, O Lord, I beseech thee how I have walked before thee in truth, and with a perfect heart, and have done that which is good in thy sight" (Isaiah 38:2). All they mean by such expressions is, that regeneration declares them to be among the servants and children to whom God engages that he will show favor. We have already seen how he declares by the Psalmist that his eyes "are upon the righteous, and his ears are open unto their cry" (Psalm 34:16; Psalm 34:16) and again by the apostle, that "whatsoever we ask of him we obtain, because we keep his commandments" (John 3:22). In these passages he does not fix a value on prayer as a meritorious work, but designs to establish the confidence of those who are conscious of an unfeigned integrity and innocence, such as all believers should possess. For the saying of the blind man who had received his sight is in perfect accordance with divine truth, And God heareth not sinners (John 9:31); provided we take the term sinners in the sense commonly used by Scripture to mean those who, without any desire for righteousness, are sleeping secure in their sins; since no heart will ever rise to genuine prayer that does not at the same time long for holiness.

Those supplications in which the saints allude to their purity and integrity correspond to such promises, that they may thus have, in their own experience, a manifestation of that which all the servants of God are made to expect. Thus they almost always use this mode of prayer when before God they compare themselves with their enemies, from whose injustice they long to be delivered by his hand. When making such comparisons, there is no wonder that they bring forward their integrity and simplicity of heart, that thus, by the justice of their cause, the Lord may be the more disposed to give them succor. We rob not the pious breast of the privilege of enjoying a consciousness of purity before the Lord, and thus feeling assured of the promises with which he comforts and supports his true worshippers, but we would have them to lay aside all thought of their own merits and found their confidence of success in prayer solely on the divine mercy.

CHAPTER 11

- *The fourth rule of prayer: a sure confidence of being heard animates us to prayer.*

- *The kind of confidence required, viz., a serious conviction of our misery, joined with sure hope.*

- *How diffidence impairs prayer.*

- *Faith is required.*

The fourth rule of prayer is, that notwithstanding of our being thus abased and truly humbled, we should be animated to pray with the sure hope of succeeding. There is, indeed, an appearance of contradiction between the two things, between a sense of the just vengeance of God and firm confidence in his favor, and yet they are perfectly accordant, if it is the mere goodness of God that raises up those who are overwhelmed by their own sins. For, as we have formerly shown that repentance and faith go hand in hand, being united by an indissoluble tie, the one causing terror, the other joy, so in prayer they must both be present. This concurrence David expresses in a few words: "But as for me, I will come into thy house in the multitude of thy mercy, and in thy fear will I worship toward thy holy temple" (Psalm 5:7). Under the goodness of God he comprehends faith, at the same time not excluding fear; for not only does his majesty compel our reverence, but our own unworthiness also divests us of all pride and confidence, and keeps us in fear.

The confidence of which I speak is not one which frees the mind from all anxiety, and soothes it with sweet and perfect rest; such rest is peculiar to those who, while all their affairs are flowing to a wish are annoyed by no care, stung with no regret, agitated by no fear. But the best stimulus which the saints have to prayer is when, in consequence of their own necessities, they feel the greatest disquietude, and are all but driven to despair, until faith seasonably comes to their aid; because in such straits the goodness of God so shines upon them, that while they groan, burdened by the weight of present calamities, and tormented with the fear of greater, they yet trust to this goodness, and in this way both lighten the difficulty of endurance, and take comfort in the hope of final deliverance. It is necessary therefore, that the prayer of the believer should be the result of both feelings, and exhibit the influence of both; namely, that while he groans under present and anxiously dreads new evils, he should, at the same times have recourse to God, not at all doubting that God is ready to stretch out a helping hand to him. For it is not easy to say how much God is irritated by our distrust, when we ask what we expect not of his goodness.

Hence, nothing is more accordant to the nature of prayer than to lay it down as a fixed rule, that it is not to come forth at random, but is to follow in the footsteps of faith. To this principle Christ directs all of us in these words, " Therefore, I say unto you, What things soever ye desire, when ye pray, believe that ye receive them, and ye shall have them" (Mark 11:24). The same thing he declares in another passage, "All things, whatsoever ye shall ask in prayer, believing, ye shall receive" (Matthew 21:22). In accordance with this are the words of James, "If any of you lack wisdom, let him ask of God, that giveth to all men liberally, and upbraideth not, and it shall be given him. But let him ask in faith, nothing wavering" (James 1:5). He most aptly expresses the power of faith by opposing it to wavering. No less worthy of notice is his additional statement, that those who approach God with a doubting, hesitating mind, without feeling assured whether they are to be heard or not, gain nothing by their prayers. Such persons he compares to a wave of the sea, driven with the wind and tossed. Hence, in another passage he terms genuine prayer "the prayer of faith" (James 5:15).

Again, since God so often declares that he will give to every man according to his faith he intimates that we cannot obtain anything without faith. In short, it is faith which obtains everything that is granted to prayer. This is the meaning of Paul in the well known passage to which dull men give too little heed, "How then shall they call upon him in whom they have not believed? and how shall they believe in him of whom they have not heard?" "So then faith cometh by hearing, and hearing by the word of God" (Romans 10:14, 17). Gradually deducing the origin of prayer from faith, he distinctly maintains that God cannot be invoked sincerely except by those to whom, by the preaching of the Gospel, his mercy and willingness have been made known, nay, familiarly explained.

CHAPTER 12

- *This faith and sure hope is regarded by our opponents as most absurd.*

- *Their error described and refuted by various passages of Scripture, which show that acceptable prayer is accompanied with these qualities.*

- *There is no repugnance between this certainty and an acknowledgment of our destitution.*

This necessity our opponents do not at all consider. Therefore, when we say that believers ought to feel firmly assured, they think we are saying the most absurd thing in the world. But if they had any experience in true prayer, they would assuredly understand that God cannot be duly invoked without this firm sense of the Divine benevolence. But as no man can well perceive the power of faith, without at the same time feeling it in his heart, what profit is there in disputing with men of this character, who plainly show that they have never had more than a vain imagination? The value and necessity of that assurance for which we contend is learned chiefly from prayer. Everyone who does not see this gives proof of a very stupid conscience. Therefore, leaving those who are thus blinded, let us fix our thoughts on the words of Paul, that God can only be invoked by such as have obtained a knowledge of his mercy from the Gospel, and feel firmly assured that that mercy is ready to be bestowed upon them. What kind of prayer would this be? "O Lord, I am indeed doubtful whether or not thou art inclined to hear me; but being oppressed with anxiety I fly to thee that if I am worthy, thou mayest assist me." None of the saints whose prayers are given in Scripture thus supplicated.

Nor are we thus taught by the Holy Spirit, who tells us to "come boldly unto the throne of grace, that we may obtain mercy, and find grace to help in time of need" (Hebrews 4:16); and elsewhere teaches us to "have boldness and access with confidence by the faith of Christ" (Ephesians 3:12). This confidence of obtaining what we ask, a confidence which the Lord commands, and all the saints teach by their example, we must therefore hold fast with both hands, if we would pray to any advantage. The only prayer acceptable to God is that which springs (if I may so express it) from this presumption of faith, and is founded on the full assurance of hope. He might have been contented to use the simple name of faith, but he adds not only confidence, but liberty or boldness, that by this mark he might distinguish us from unbelievers, who indeed like us pray to God, but pray at random. Hence, the whole Church thus prays "Let thy mercy O Lord, be upon us, according as we hope in thee" (Psalm 33:22).

The same condition is set down by the Psalmist in another passage, "When I cry unto thee, then shall mine enemies turn back: this I know, for God is for me" (Psalm 56:9). Again, "In the morning will I direct my prayer unto thee, and will look up" (Psalm 5:3). From these words we gather, that prayers are vainly poured out into the air unless accompanied with faith, in which, as from a watchtower, we may quietly wait for God. With this agrees the order of Paul's exhortation. For before urging believers to pray in the Spirit always, with vigilance and assiduity, he enjoins them to take "the shield of faith," "the helmet of salvation, and the sword of the Spirit, which is the word of God" (Ephesians 6:16-18).

Let the reader here call to mind what I formerly observed, that faith by no means fails though accompanied with a recognition of our wretchedness, poverty, and pollution. How much soever believers may feel that they are oppressed by a heavy load of iniquity, and are not only devoid of everything which can procure the favor of God for them, but justly burdened with many sins which make him an object of dread, yet they cease not to present themselves, this feeling not deterring them from appearing in his presence, because there is no other access to him.

Genuine prayer is not that by which we arrogantly extol ourselves before God, or set a great value on anything of our own, but that by which, while confessing our guilt, we utter our sorrows before God, just as children familiarly lay their complaints before their parents. Nay, the immense accumulation of our sins should rather spur us on and incite us to prayer. Of this the Psalmist gives us an example, "Heal my soul: for I have sinned against thee" (Psalm 41:4). I confess, indeed, that these stings would prove mortal darts, did not God give succor; but our heavenly Father has, in ineffable kindness, added a remedy, by which, calming all perturbation, soothing our cares, and dispelling our fears he condescendingly allures us to himself; nay, removing all doubts, not to say obstacles, makes the way smooth before us.

CHAPTER 13

- *To our unworthiness we oppose:*

    a. The command of God.

    b. The promise.

- *Rebels and hypocrites are completely condemned.*

- *Passages of Scripture confirming the command to pray.*

And first, indeed in enjoining us to pray, he by the very injunction convicts us of impious contumacy if we obey not. He could not give a more precise command than that which is contained in the psalms: "Call upon me in the day of trouble" (Psalm 50:15). But as there is no office of piety more frequently enjoined by Scripture, there is no occasion for here dwelling longer upon it. "Ask," says our Divine Master, "and it shall be given you; seek, and ye shall find; knock, and it shall be opened unto you" (Matthew 7:7). Here, indeed, a promise is added to the precept, and this is necessary. For though all confess that we must obey the precept, yet the greater part would shun the invitation of God, did he not promise that he would listen and be ready to answer.

These two positions being laid down, it is certain that all who cavillingly [finding fault unnecessarily; raising trivial objections] allege that they are not to come to God directly, are not only rebellious and disobedient but are also convicted of unbelief, inasmuch as they distrust the promises. There is the more occasion to attend to this, because hypocrites, under a pretense of humility and modesty, proudly contemn the precept, as well as deny all credit to the gracious invitation of God; nay, rob him of a principal part of his worship. For when he rejected sacrifices, in which all holiness seemed then to consist, he declared that the chief thing, that which above all others is precious in his sight, is to be invoked in the day of necessity. Therefore, when he demands that which is his own, and urges us to alacrity in obeying, no pretexts for doubt, how specious soever they may be, can excuse us.

Hence, all the passages throughout Scripture in which we are commanded to pray, are set up before our eyes as so many banners, to inspire us with confidence. It were presumption to go forward into the presence of God, did he not anticipate us by his invitation. Accordingly, he opens up the way for us by his own voice, "I will say, It is my people: and they shall say, The Lord is my God" (Zechariah 13:9). We see how he anticipates his worshippers, and desires them to follow, and therefore we cannot fear that the melody which he himself dictates will prove unpleasing. Especially let us call to mind that noble description of the divine character, by trusting to which we shall easily overcome every obstacle: O thou that hearest prayer, unto thee shall all flesh come" (Psalm 65:2). What can be more lovely or soothing than to see God invested with a title which assures us that nothing is more proper to his nature than to listen to the prayers of suppliants? Hence the Psalmist infers, that free access is given not to a few individuals, but to all men, since God addresses all in these terms, "Call upon me in the day of trouble: I will deliver thee, and thou shalt glorify me" (Psalm 50:15). David, accordingly, appeals to the promise thus given in order to obtain what he asks: "Thou, O Lord of hosts, God of Israel, hast revealed to thy servant, saying, I will build thee an house: therefore hath thy servant found in his heart to pray this prayer unto thee" (2 Samuel 7:27). Here we infer, that he would have been afraid but for the promise which emboldened him. So in another passage he fortifies himself with the general doctrine, "He will fulfill the desire of them that fear him" (Psalm 145:19).

Nay, we may observe in the Psalms how the continuity of prayer is broken, and a transition is made at one time to the power of God, at another to his goodness, at another to the faithfulness of his promises. It might seem that David, by introducing these sentiments, unseasonably mutilates his prayers; but believers well know by experience, that their ardor grows languid unless new fuel is added, and, therefore, that meditation as well on the nature as on the word of God during prayer, is by no means superfluous. Let us imitate the example of David, and introduce thoughts which may reanimate our languid minds with new vigor.

CHAPTER 14

- *Additional passages concerning the promises which belong to the pious when they invoke God.*

- *These promises are realized provided we indulge no vain confidence, and sincerely cast ourselves upon the mercy of God.*

- *Those who do not invoke God under urgent necessity are no better than idolaters.*

- *This concurrence of fear and confidence reconciles the different passages of Scripture, as to humbling ourselves in prayer, and causing our prayers to ascend.*

It is strange that these delightful promises affect us coldly, or scarcely at all, so that the generality of men prefer to wander up and down, forsaking the fountain of living waters, and hewing out to themselves broken cisterns, rather than embrace the divine liberality voluntarily offered to them (Jeremiah 2:13). "The name of the Lord," says Solomon, "is a strong tower; the righteous runneth into it, and is safe." (Proverbs 18:10) Joel, after predicting the fearful disaster which was at hand, subjoins the following memorable sentence: " And it shall come to pass, that whosoever shall call on the name of the Lord shall be delivered." (Joel 2:32) This we know properly refers to the course of the Gospel. Scarcely one in a hundred is moved to come into the presence of God, though he himself exclaims by Isaiah, "And it shall come to pass, that before they call, I will answer; and while they are yet speaking, I will hear." (Isaiah 65:24) This honor he elsewhere bestows upon the whole Church in general, as belonging to all the members of Christ: "He shall call upon me, and I will answer him: I will be with him in trouble; I will deliver him, and honor him." (Psalm 91:15) My intention, however, as I already observed, is not to enumerate all, but only select some admirable passages as a specimen how kindly God allures us to himself, and how extreme our ingratitude must be when with such powerful motives our sluggishness still retards us. Wherefore, let these words always resound in our ears: "The Lord is nigh unto all them that call upon him, to all that call upon him in truth" (Psalm 145:18).

Likewise those passages which we have quoted from Isaiah and Joel, in which God declares that his ear is open to our prayers, and that he is delighted as with a sacrifice of sweet savor when we cast our cares upon him. The special benefit of these promises we receive when we frame our prayer, not timorously or doubtingly, but when trusting to his word whose majesty might otherwise deter us, we are bold to call him Father, he himself deigning to suggest this most delightful name. Fortified by such invitations it remains for us to know that we have therein sufficient materials for prayer, since our prayers depend on no merit of our own, but all their worth and hope of success are founded and depend on the promises of God, so that they need no other support, and require not to look up and down on this hand and on that.

It must therefore be fixed in our minds, that though we equal not the lauded sanctity of patriarchs, prophets, and apostles, yet as the command to pray is common to us as well as them, and faith is common, so if we lean on the word of God, we are in respect of this privilege their associates. For God declaring, as has already been seen, that he will listen and be favorable to all, encourages the most wretched to hope that they shall obtain what they ask; and, accordingly, we should attend to the general forms of expression, which, as it is commonly expressed, exclude none from first to last; only let there be sincerity of heart, self-dissatisfaction, humility, and faith, that we may not, by the hypocrisy of a deceitful prayer, profane the name of God.

Our most merciful Father will not reject those whom he not only encourages to come, but urges in every possible way. Hence David's method of prayer to which I lately referred: "And now, O Lord God, thou art that God, and thy words be true, and thou hast promised this goodness unto thy servant, that it may continue forever before thee" (2 Samuel 7:28). So also, in another passage, "Let, I pray thee, thy merciful kindness be for my comfort, according to thy word unto thy servant" (Psalm 119:76). And the whole body of the Israelites, whenever they fortify themselves with the remembrance of the covenant, plainly declare, that since God thus prescribes they are not to pray timorously (Genesis 32:13). In this they imitated the example of the patriarchs, particularly Jacob, who, after confessing that he was unworthy of the many mercies which he had received of the Lord's hand, says, that he is encouraged to make still larger requests, because God had promised that he would grant them. But whatever be the pretexts which unbelievers employ, when they do not flee to God as often as necessity urges, nor seek after him, nor implore his aid, they defraud him of his due honor just as much as if they were fabricating to themselves new gods and idols, since in this way they deny that God is the author of all their blessings.

On the contrary, nothing more effectually frees pious minds from every doubt, than to be armed with the thought that no obstacle should impede them while they are obeying the command of God, who declares that nothing is more grateful to him than obedience. Hence, again, what I have previously said becomes still more clear, namely, that a bold spirit in prayer well accords with fear, reverence, and anxiety, and that there is no inconsistency when God raises up those who had fallen prostrate. In this way forms of expression apparently inconsistent admirably harmonize. Jeremiah and David speak of humbly laying their supplications[5] before God (Jereremiah 42:9; Daniel 9:18). In another passage Jeremiah says "Let, we beseech thee, our supplication be accepted before thee, and pray for us unto the Lord thy God, even for all this remnant" (Jeremiah 42:2). On the other hand, believers are often said to lift up prayer.

Thus Hezekiah speaks, when asking the prophet to undertake the office of interceding (2 Kings 19:4). And David says, "Let my prayer

---

[5] Latin, "prosternere preces." French, "mettent bas leurs prieres;"

  --lay low their prayers.

be set forth before thee as incense; and the lifting up of my hands as the evening sacrifice" (Psalm 141:2). The explanation is, that though believers, persuaded of the paternal love of God, cheerfully rely on his faithfulness, and have no hesitation in imploring the aid which he voluntarily offers, they are not elated with supine or presumptuous security; but climbing up by the ladder of the promises, still remain humble and abased suppliants.

CHAPTER 15

- *Some prayers have proved effectual, though not according to the form prescribed. Such examples, though not given for our imitation, are of the greatest use.*

- *But aren't the prayers of the faithful sometimes not effectual? Answered by a noble passage of Augustine.*

- *Rule for right prayer.*

Here, by way of objection, several questions are raised. Scripture relates that God sometimes complied with certain prayers which had been dictated by minds not duly calmed or regulated. It is true, that the cause for which Jotham imprecated on the inhabitants of Shechem the disaster which afterwards befell them was well founded; but still he was inflamed with anger and revenge (Judges 9:20); and hence God, by complying with the execration, seems to approve of passionate impulses. Similar fervor also seized Samson, when he prayed, " Strengthen me, I pray thee, only this once, O God, that I may be at once avenged of the Philistines for my two eyes" (Judges 16:28). For although there was some mixture of good zeal, yet his ruling feeling was a fervent, and therefore vicious longing for vengeance. God assents, and hence apparently it might be inferred that prayers are effectual, though not framed in conformity to the rule of the word.

But I answer, first, that a perpetual law is not abrogated by singular examples; and, secondly, that special suggestions have sometimes been made to a few individuals, whose case thus becomes different from that of the generality of men. For we should attend to the answer which our Savior gave to his disciples when they inconsiderately wished to imitate the example of Elias, "Ye know not what manner of spirit ye are of" (Luke 9:55). We must, however, go farther and say, that the wishes to which God assents are not always pleasing to him; but he assents, because it is necessary, by way of example, to give clear evidence of the doctrine of Scripture, viz., that he assists the miserable, and hears the groans of those who unjustly afflicted implore his aid: and, accordingly, he executes his judgments when the complaints of the needy, though in themselves unworthy of attention, ascend to him. For how often, in inflicting punishment on the ungodly for cruelty, rapine, violence, lust, and other crimes, in curbing audacity and fury, and also in overthrowing tyrannical power, has he declared that he gives assistance to those who are unworthily oppressed though they by addressing an unknown deity only beat the air?

There is one psalm which clearly teaches that prayers are not without effect, though they do not penetrate to heaven by faith (Psalm 107:6, 13, 19). For it enumerates the prayers which, by natural instinct, necessity extorts from unbelievers not less than from believers, and to which it shows by the event, that God is, notwithstanding, propitious. Is it to testify by such readiness to hear that their prayers are agreeable to him? Nay; it is, first, to magnify or display his mercy by the circumstance, that even the wishes of unbelievers are not denied; and, secondly, to stimulate his true worshippers to more urgent prayer, when they see that sometimes even the wailings of the ungodly are not without avail. This, however, is no reason why believers should deviate from the law divinely imposed upon them, or envy unbelievers, as if they gained much in obtaining what they wished. We have observed that in this way God yielded to the feigned repentance of Ahab, that he might show how ready he is to listen to his elect when, with true contrition, they seek his favor. Accordingly, he upbraids the Jews, that shortly after experiencing his readiness to listen to their prayers, they returned to their own perverse inclinations. It is also plain from the Book of Judges that, whenever they wept, though their tears were deceitful, they were delivered from the hands of their enemies. Therefore, as God sends his sun indiscriminately on the evil and on the good, so he despises not the tears of those who have a good cause, and whose sorrows are deserving of relief. Meanwhile, though he hears them, it has no more to do with salvation than the supply of food which he gives to other despisers of his goodness.

There seems to be a more difficult question concerning Abraham and Samuel, the one of whom, without any instruction from the word of God, prayed in behalf of the people of Sodom, and the other, contrary to an express prohibition, prayed in behalf of Saul (Genesis 18:23; 1 Samuel 15:11). Similar is the case of Jeremiah, who prayed that the city might not be destroyed (Jeremiah 32:16 ff). It is true their prayers were refused, but it seems harsh to affirm that they prayed without faith. Modest readers will, I hope, be satisfied with this solution, viz., that leaning to the general principle on which God enjoins us to be merciful even to the unworthy, they were not altogether devoid of faith, though in this particular instance their wish was disappointed. Augustine shrewdly remarks, "How do the saints pray in faith when they ask from God contrary to what he has decreed? Namely, because they pray according to his will, not his hidden and immutable will, but that which he suggests to them, that he may hear them in another manner; as he wisely distinguishes" (Augustine *The City of God*, book 22, chapter 2). This is truly said: for, in his incomprehensible counsel, he so regulates events, that the prayers of the saints, though involving a mixture of faith and error, are not in vain.

And yet this no more sanctions imitation than it excuses the saints themselves, who I deny not exceeded due bounds. Wherefore, whenever no certain promise exists, our request to God must have a condition annexed to it. Here we may refer to the prayer of David, "Awake for me to the judgment that thou hast commanded" (Psalm 7:6); for he reminds us that he had received special instruction to pray for a temporal blessing[6].

---

[6] The French adds, "duquel id n'eust pas autrement esté asseuré;"--of which he would not otherwise have felt assured.

CHAPTER 16

- *The above four rules of prayer are not so rigid that every prayer deficient in them in any respect is rejected by God.*

- *Concluding summary of this section.*

It is also of importance to observe, that the four laws of prayer of which I have treated are not so rigorously enforced, as that God rejects the prayers in which he does not find perfect faith or repentance, accompanied with fervent zeal and wishes duly framed. We have said (sec. 4), that though prayer is the familiar intercourse of believers with God, yet reverence and modesty must be observed: we must not give loose reins to our wishes, nor long for anything farther than God permits; and, moreover, lest the majesty of God should be despised, our minds must be elevated to pure and chaste veneration. This no man ever performed with due perfection.

For, not to speak of the generality of men, how often do David's complaints savor of intemperance? Not that he actually means to expostulate with God, or murmur at his judgments, but failing, through infirmity, he finds no better solace than to pour his griefs into the bosom of his heavenly Father. Nay, even our stammering is tolerated by God, and pardon is granted to our ignorance as often as anything rashly escapes us: indeed, without this indulgence, we should have no freedom to pray. But although it was David's intention to submit himself entirely to the will of God, and he prayed with no less patience than fervor, yet irregular emotions appear, nay, sometimes burst forth, -- emotions not a little at variance with the first law which we laid down. In particular, we may see in a clause of the thirty-ninth Psalm, how this saint was carried away by the vehemence of his grief, and unable to keep within bounds. "O spare me[7], that I may recover

---

[7] Latin, "Desine a me." French, "Retire-toy;"--Withdraw from me.

strength, before I go hence, and be no more" (Psalm 39:13). You would call this the language of a desperate man, who had no other desire than that God should withdraw and leave him to relish in his distresses. Not that his devout mind rushes into such intemperance, or that, as the reprobate are wont, he wishes to have done with God; he only complains that the divine anger is more than he can bear. During those trials, wishes often escape which are not in accordance with the rule of the word, and in which the saints do not duly consider what is lawful and expedient.

Prayers contaminated by such faults, indeed, deserve to be rejected; yet provided the saints lament, administer self-correction and return to themselves, God pardons. Similar faults are committed in regard to the second law (as to which, see chapter 6), for the saints have often to struggle with their own coldness, their want and misery not urging them sufficiently to serious prayer. It often happens, also, that their minds wander, and are almost lost; hence in this matter also there is need of pardon, lest their prayers, from being languid or mutilated, or interrupted and wandering, should meet with a refusal.

One of the natural feelings which God has imprinted on our mind is that prayer is not genuine unless the thoughts are turned upward. Hence the ceremony of raising the hands, to which we have adverted, a ceremony known to all ages and nations, and still in common use. But who, in lifting up his hands, is not conscious of sluggishness, the heart cleaving to the earth? In regard to the petition for remission of sins (chapter 8), though no believer omits it, yet all who are truly exercised in prayer feel that they bring scarcely a tenth of the sacrifice of which David speaks, "The sacrifices of God are a broken spirit: a broken and a contrite heart, O God, thou wilt not despise" (Psalm 51:17). Thus a twofold pardon is always to be asked; first, because they are conscious of many faults the sense of which, however, does not touch them so as to make them feel dissatisfied with themselves as they ought; and, secondly, in so far as they have been enabled to profit in repentance and the fear of God, they are humbled with just sorrow for their offenses, and pray for the remission of punishment by the judge. The thing which most of all vitiates prayer, did not God indulgently interpose, is weakness or imperfection of faith; but it is not wonderful that this defect is pardoned by God, who often exercises his people with severe trials, as if he actually wished to extinguish their faith.

The hardest of such trials is when believers are forced to exclaim, "O Lord God of hosts, how long wilt thou be angry against the prayer of thy people?" (Psalm 80:4), as if their very prayers offended him. In like manner, when Jeremiah says "Also when I cry and shout, he shutteth out my prayers (Lamentations 3:8), there cannot be a doubt that he was in the greatest perturbation. Innumerable examples of the same kind occur in the Scriptures, from which it is manifest that the faith of the saints was often mingled with doubts and fears, so that while believing and hoping, they, however, betrayed some degree of unbelief. But because they do not come so far as were to be wished, that is only an additional reason for their exerting themselves to correct their faults, that they may daily approach nearer to the perfect law of prayer, and at the same time feel into what an abyss of evils those are plunged, who, in the very cures they use, bring new diseases upon themselves: since there is no prayer which God would not deservedly disdain, did he not overlook the blemishes with which all of them are polluted. I do not mention these things that believers may securely pardon themselves in any faults which they commit, but that they may call themselves to strict account, and thereby endeavor to surmount these obstacles; and though Satan endeavors to block up all the paths in order to prevent them from praying, they may, nevertheless, break through, being firmly persuaded that though not disencumbered of all hindrances, their attempts are pleasing to God, and their wishes are approved, provided they hasten on and keep their aim, though without immediately reaching it.

CHAPTER 17

- *God is to be invoked only through Jesus.*

- *This truth is founded on a consideration of the divine majesty, and the precept and promise of God himself.*

But since no man is worthy to come forward in his own name, and appear in the presence of God, our heavenly Father, to relieve us at once from fear and shame, with which all must feel oppressed[8], has given us his Son, Jesus Christ our Lord, to be our Advocate and Mediator, that under his guidance we may approach securely, confiding that with him for our Intercessor nothing which we ask in his name will be denied to us, as there is nothing which the Father can deny to him (1 Timothy 2:5; 1 John 2:1; see sec. 36, 37). To this it is necessary to refer all that we have previously taught concerning faith; because, as the promise gives us Christ as our Mediator, so, unless our hope of obtaining what we ask is founded on him, it deprives us of the privilege of prayer. For it is impossible to think of the dread majesty of God without being filled with alarm; and hence the sense of our own unworthiness must keep us far away, until Christ interpose, and convert a throne of dreadful glory into a throne of grace, as the Apostle teaches that thus we can "come boldly unto the throne of grace, that we may obtain mercy, and find grace to help in time of need" (Hebrews 4:16).

And as a rule has been laid down as to prayer, as a promise has been given that those who pray will be heard, so we are specially enjoined to pray in the name of Christ, the promise being that we shall obtain what we ask in his name. "Whatsoever ye shall ask in my name," says our Savior, "that will I do; that the Father may be glorified in the

---

[8] French, "Confusion que nous avons, ou devons avoir en nousmesmes;"--confusion which we have, or ought to have, in ourselves.

Son;" "Hitherto ye have asked nothing in my name; ask, and ye shall receive, that your joy may be full" (John 14:13; 16:24). Hence it is incontrovertibly clear that those who pray to God in any other name than that of Christ contumaciously falsify his orders, and regard his will as nothing, while they have no promise that they shall obtain. For, as Paul says "All the promises of God in him are yea, and in him amen;" (2 Corinthians 1:20), that is, are confirmed and fulfilled in him.

CHAPTER 18

- *From the first all believers were heard through him only, yet this was especially restricted to the period subsequent to his ascension.*

- *The reason for this restriction.*

And we must carefully attend to the circumstance of time. Christ enjoins his disciples to have recourse to his intercession after he shall have ascended to heaven: "At that day ye shall ask in my name" (John 16:26). It is certain, indeed, that from the very first all who ever prayed were heard only for the sake of the Mediator. For this reason God had commanded in the Law, that the priest alone should enter the sanctuary, bearing the names of the twelve tribes of Israel on his shoulders, and as many precious stones on his breast, while the people were to stand at a distance in the outer court, and thereafter unite their prayers with the priest. Nay, the sacrifice had even the effect of ratifying and confirming their prayers. That shadowy ceremony of the Law therefore taught, first, that we are all excluded from the face of God, and, therefore, that there is need of a Mediator to appear in our name, and carry us on his shoulders and keep us bound upon his breast, that we may be heard in his person; And secondly, that our prayers, which, as has been said, would otherwise never be free from impurity, are cleansed by the sprinkling of his blood. And we see that the saints, when they desired to obtain anything, founded their hopes on sacrifices, because they knew that by sacrifice all prayers were ratified: "Remember all thy offerings," says David, "and accept thy burnt sacrifice" (Psalm 20:3).

Hence we infer, that in receiving the prayers of his people, God was from the very first appeased by the intercession of Christ. Why then does Christ speak of a new period ("at that day") when the disciples were to begin to pray in his name, unless it be that this grace, being now more brightly displayed, ought also to be in higher estimation with us? In this sense he had said a little before, "Hitherto ye have asked nothing in my name; ask." Not that they were altogether ignorant of the office of Mediator (all the Jews were instructed in these first rudiments), but they did not clearly understand that Christ by his ascent to heaven would be more the advocate of the Church than before. Therefore, to solace their grief for his absence by some more than ordinary result, he asserts his office of advocate, and says, that hitherto they had been without the special benefit which it would be their privilege to enjoy, when aided by his intercession they should invoke God with greater freedom.

In this sense the Apostle says that we have "boldness to enter into the holiest by the blood of Jesus, by a new and living way, which he hath consecrated for us" (Hebrews 10:19, 20). Therefore, the more inexcusable we are, if we do not with both hands (as it is said) embrace the inestimable gift which is properly destined for us.

CHAPTER 19

- *The wrath of God lies upon those who reject Christ as Mediator.*

- *This does not exclude the mutual intercession of saints on the earth.*

Moreover since he himself is the only way and the only access by which we can draw near to God, those who deviate from this way, and decline this access, have no other remaining; his throne presents nothing but wrath, judgment, and terror. In short, as the Father has consecrated him our guide and head, those who abandon or turn aside from him in any way endeavor, as much as in them lies, to sully and efface the stamp which God has impressed. Christ, therefore, is the only Mediator by whose intercession the Father is rendered propitious and exorable (1 Timothy 2:5).

For though the saints are still permitted to use intercessions, by which they mutually beseech God in behalf of each other's salvation, and of which the Apostle makes mention (Ephesians 6:18, 19; 1 Timothy 2:1); yet these depend on that one intercession, so far are they from derogating from it. For as the intercessions which, as members of one body we offer up for each other, spring from the feeling of love, so they have reference to this one head. Being thus also made in the name of Christ, what more do they than declare that no man can derive the least benefit from any prayers without the intercession of Christ? As there is nothing in the intercession of Christ to prevent the different members of the Church from offering up prayers for each other, so let it be held as a fixed principle, that all the intercessions thus used in the Church must have reference to that one intercession.

Nay, we must be especially careful to show our gratitude on this very account, that God pardoning our unworthiness, not only allows each individual to pray for himself, but allows all to intercede mutually for each other. God having given a place in his Church to intercessors who would deserve to be rejected when praying privately on their own account, how presumptuous were it to abuse this kindness by employing it to obscure the honor of Christ?

CHAPTER 20

- *Refutation of errors interfering with the intercession of Christ.*

    a. Christ is the Mediator of redemption

    b. The saints are mediators of intercession.

- *Answer confirmed by the clear testimony of Scripture, and by a passage from Augustine.*

- *The nature of Christ's intercession.*

Moreover, the Sophists are guilty of the merest trifling when they allege that Christ is the Mediator of redemption, but that believers are mediators of intercession; as if Christ had only performed a temporary mediation, and left an eternal and imperishable mediation to his servants. Such, forsooth, is the treatment which he receives from those who pretend only to take from him a minute portion of honor.

Very different is the language of Scripture, with whose simplicity every pious man will be satisfied, without paying any regard to those importers. For when John says, "If any man sin, we have an advocate with the Father, Jesus Christ the righteous" (1 John 2:1), does he mean merely that we once had an advocate; does he not rather ascribe to him a perpetual intercession? What does Paul mean when he declares that he "is even at the right hand of God, who also maketh intercession for us"? (Romans 8:32). But when in another passage he declares that he is the only Mediator between God and man (1 Timothy 2:5), is he not referring to the supplications which he had mentioned a little before? Having previously said that prayers were to be offered up for all men, he immediately adds, in confirmation of that statement, that there is one God, and one Mediator between God and man.

Nor does Augustine give a different interpretation when he says, "Christian men mutually recommend each other in their prayers. But

106

he for whom none intercedes, while he himself intercedes for all, is the only true Mediator. Though the Apostle Paul was under the head a principal member, yet because he was a member of the body of Christ, and knew that the most true and High Priest of the Church had entered not by figure into the inner veil to the holy of holies, but by firm and express truth into the inner sanctuary of heaven to holiness, holiness not imaginary, but eternal (Hebrews 9:11, 24), he also commends himself to the prayers of the faithful (Romans 15:30; Ephesians 6:19; Colossians 4:3). He does not make himself a mediator between God and the people, but asks that all the members of the body of Christ should pray mutually for each other, since the members are mutually sympathetic: if one member suffers, the others suffer with it (1 Corinthians 12:26). And thus the mutual prayers of all the members still laboring on the earth ascend to the Head, who has gone before into heaven, and in whom there is propitiation for our sins. For if Paul were a mediator, so would also the other apostles, and thus there would be many mediators, and Paul's statement could not stand, 'There is one God, and one Mediator between God and men, the man Christ Jesus;' (1 Timothy 2:5) in whom we also are one (Romans 12:5) if we keep the unity of the faith in the bond of peace (Ephesians 4:3)," (Augustine, *Against the Letter of Parmenian*, book 2, chapter 8). Likewise in another passage Augustine says, "If thou requirest a priest, he is above the heavens, where he intercedes for those who on earth died for thee" (Augustine in Psalm 94). We imagine not that he throws himself before his Father's knees, and suppliantly intercedes for us; but we understand with the Apostle, that he appears in the presence of God, and that the power of his death has the effect of a perpetual intercession for us; that having entered into the upper sanctuary, he alone continues to the end of the world to present the prayers of his people, who are standing far off in the outer court.

CHAPTER 21

• *Of the intercession of saints living with Christ in heaven.*

   a. Fiction of the Papists in regard to it.

   b. Its absurdity.

   c. It is nowhere mentioned by Scripture.

   d. Appeal to the conscience of the superstitious.

• *Its blasphemy.*

• *Exception. Answers.*

In regard to the saints who having died in the body live in Christ, if we attribute prayer to them, let us not imagine that they have any other way of supplicating God than through Christ who alone is the way, or that their prayers are accepted by God in any other name. Wherefore, since the Scripture calls us away from all others to Christ alone, since our heavenly Father is pleased to gather together all things in him, it were the extreme of stupidity, not to say madness, to attempt to obtain access by means of others, so as to be drawn away from him without whom access cannot be obtained. But who can deny that this was the practice for several ages, and is still the practice, wherever Popery prevails?

To procure the favor of God, human merits are ever and anon obtruded, and very frequently while Christ is passed by, God is supplicated in their name. I ask if this is not to transfer to them that office of sole intercession which we have above claimed for Christ? Then what angel or devil ever announced one syllable to any human being concerning that fancied intercession of theirs? There is not a word on the subject in Scripture. What ground then was there for the fiction? Certainly, while the human mind thus seeks help for itself in which it is not sanctioned by the word of God, it plainly manifests its distrust (see chapter 27). But if we appeal to the consciences of all who take pleasure in the intercession of saints, we shall find that their only reason for it is, that they are filled with anxiety, as if they supposed that Christ were insufficient or too rigorous. By this anxiety they dishonor Christ, and rob him of his title of sole Mediator, a title which being given him by the Father as his special privilege, ought not to be transferred to any other. By so doing they obscure the glory of his nativity and make void his cross; in short, divest and defraud of due praise everything which he did or suffered, since all which he did and suffered goes to show that he is and ought to be deemed sole Mediator.

At the same time, they reject the kindness of God in manifesting himself to them as a Father, for he is not their Father if they do not recognize Christ as their brother. This they plainly refuse to do if they think not that he feels for them a brother's affection; affection than which none can be more gentle or tender. Wherefore Scripture offers him alone, sends us to him, and establishes us in him. "He," says Ambrose, "is our mouth by which we speak to the Father; our eye by which we see the Father; our right hand by which we offer ourselves to the Father. Save by his intercession neither we nor any saints have any intercourse with God" (Ambrose, *On Isaac and the Soul*).

If they object that the public prayers which are offered up in churches conclude with the words, through Jesus Christ our Lord, it is a frivolous evasion; because no less insult is offered to the intercession of Christ by confounding it with the prayers and merits of the dead, than by omitting it altogether, and making mention only of the dead. Then, in all their litanies, hymns, and prose where every kind of honor is paid to dead saints, there is no mention of Christ.

CHAPTER 22

- *The monstrous errors resulting from this fiction.*

- *An exception by the advocates of this fiction answered.*

But here stupidity has proceeded to such a length as to give a manifestation of the genius of superstition, which, when once it has shaken off the rein, is wont to wanton without limit. After men began to look to the intercession of saints, a peculiar administration was gradually assigned to each, so that, according to diversity of business, now one, now another, intercessor was invoked. Then individuals adopted particular saints, and put their faith in them, just as if they had been tutelary deities. And thus not only were gods set up according to the number of the cities (the charge which the prophet brought against Israel of old, Jeremiah 2:28; 11:13), but according to the number of individuals. But while the saints in all their desires refer to the will of God alone, look to it, and acquiesce in it, yet to assign to them any other prayer than that of longing for the arrival of the kingdom of God, is to think of them stupidly, carnally, and even insultingly. Nothing can be farther from such a view than to imagine that each, under the influence of private feeling, is disposed to be most favorable to his own worshippers.

At length vast numbers have fallen into the horrid blasphemy of invoking them not merely as helping but presiding over their salvation. See the depth to which miserable men fall when they forsake their proper station, that is, the word of God. I say nothing of the more monstrous specimens of impiety in which, though detestable to God, angels, and men, they themselves feel no pain or shame. Prostrated at a statue or picture of Barbara or Catherine, and the like, they mutter an Our Father[9] and so far are their pastors[10] from curing or curbing this frantic course, that, allured by the scent of gain, they approve and applaud it. But while seeking to relieve themselves of the odium of this vile and criminal procedure, with what pretext can they defend the practice of calling upon Eloy (Eligius) or Medard to look upon their servants, and send them help from heaven, or the Holy Virgin to order her Son to do what they ask[11]?

The Council of Carthage forbade direct prayer to be made at the altar to saints. It is probable that these holy men, unable entirely to suppress the force of depraved custom, had recourse to this check, that public prayers might not be vitiated with such forms of expression as "Sancte Petre, ora pro nobis" – "St. Peter, pray for us." But how much farther has this devilish extravagance proceeded when men hesitate not to transfer to the dead the peculiar attributes of Christ and God?

---

[9] Erasmus, though stumbling and walking blindfold in clear light, ventures to write thus in a letter to Sadolet, 1530: "Primum, constat nullum esse locum in divinis voluminibus, qui permittat invocare divos nisi fortasse detorquere huc placet, quod dives in Evangelica parabola implorat opem Abrahae. Quanquam autem in re tanta novare quicquam praeter auctoritatem Scripturae, merito periculosum videri possit, tamen invocationem divorum nusquam improbo," etc.--First, it is clear that there is no passage in the Sacred Volume which permits the invocation of saints, unless we are pleased to wrest to this purpose what is said in the parable as to the rich man imploring the help of Abraham. But though in so weighty a matter it may justly seem dangerous to introduce anything without the authority of Scripture, I by no means condemn the invocation of saints, etc.

[10] Latin, "Pastores;"--French, "ceux qui se disent prelats, curés, ou precheurs;"--those who call themselves prelates, curates, or preachers.

[11] French, "Mais encore qu'ils taschent de laver leur mains d'un si vilain sacrilege, d'autant qu'il ne se commet point en leurs messes ni en leurs vespres; sous quelle couleur defendront ils ces blasphemes qu'il lisent a pleine gorge, où ils prient St. Eloy ou St. Medard, de regarder du ciel leurs serviteurs pour les aider? mesmes ou ils supplient la vierge Marie de commander a son fils qu'il leur ottroye leur requestes?"--But although they endeavor to wash their hands of the vile sacrilege, inasmuch as it is not committed in their masses or vespers, under what pretext will they defend those blasphemies which they repeat with full throat, in which they pray St. Eloy or St. Medard to look from heaven upon their servants and assist them; even supplicate the Virgin Mary to command her Son to grant their requests?

CHAPTER 23

- *A refutation of arguments from the Papists for the ntercession of saints:*

  a. From the duty and office of angels.

  b. From an expression of Jeremiah respecting Moses and Samuel.

  c. The meaning of the prophet confirmed by a similar passage in Ezekiel, and the testimony of an apostle.

  d. From the nature of charity, which is more perfect in the saints in glory.

In endeavoring to prove that such intercession derives some support from Scripture they labor in vain. We frequently read (they say) of the prayers of angels, and not only so, but the prayers of believers are said to be carried into the presence of God by their hands. But if they would compare saints who have departed this life with angels, it will be necessary to prove that saints are ministering spirits, to whom has been delegated the office of superintending our salvation, to whom has been assigned the province of guiding us in all our ways, of encompassing, admonishing, and comforting us, of keeping watch over us. All these are assigned to angels, but none of them to saints. How preposterously they confound departed saints with angels is sufficiently apparent from the many different offices by which Scripture distinguishes the one from the other. No one unless admitted will presume to perform the office of pleader before an earthly judge; whence then have worms such license as to obtrude themselves on God as intercessors, while no such office has been assigned them? God has been pleased to give angels the charge of our safety. Hence they attend our sacred meetings, and the Church is to them a theatre in which they behold the manifold wisdom of God (Ephesians 3:10). Those who transfer to others this office which is peculiar to them, certainly pervert and confound the order which has been established by God and ought to be inviolable.

With similar dexterity they proceed to quote other passages. God said to Jeremiah, "Though Moses and Samuel stood before me, yet my mind could not be toward this people" (Jeremiah 15:1). How (they ask) could he have spoken thus of the dead but because he knew that they interceded for the living? My inference, on the contrary, is this: since it thus appears that neither Moses nor Samuel interceded for the people of Israel, there was then no intercession for the dead. For who of the saints can be supposed to labor for the salvation of the peoples while Moses who, when in life, far surpassed all others in this matter, does nothing? Therefore, if they persist in the paltry quibble, that the dead intercede for the living, because the Lord said, "If they stood before me," (*intercesserint*), I will argue far more speciously in this way: Moses, of whom it is said, "if he interceded," did not intercede for the people in their extreme necessity: it is probable, therefore, that no other saint intercedes, all being far behind Moses in humanity, goodness, and paternal solicitude. Thus all they gain by their cavilling is to be wounded by the very arms with which they deem themselves admirably protected. But it is very ridiculous to wrest this simple sentence in this manner; for the Lord only declares that he would not spare the iniquities of the people, though some Moses or Samuel, to whose prayers he had shown himself so indulgent, should intercede for them.

This meaning is most clearly elicited from a similar passage in Ezekiel: "Though these three men, Noah, Daniel, and Job, were in it, they should deliver but their own souls by their righteousness, saith the Lord God" (Ezekiel 14:14). Here there can be no doubt that we are to understand the words as if it had been said, If two of the persons named were again to come alive; for the third was still living, namely, Daniel, who it is well known had then in the bloom of youth given an incomparable display of piety.

Let us therefore leave out those whom Scripture declares to have completed their course. Accordingly, when Paul speaks of David, he says not that by his prayers he assisted posterity, but only that he "served his own generation" (Acts 13:36).

CHAPTER 24

- *A refutation of arguments from the Papists for the intercession of saints, continued:*

They again object, "Are those, then, to be deprived of every pious wish, who, during the whole course of their lives, breathed nothing but piety and mercy?" I have no wish curiously to pry into what they do or meditate; but the probability is, that instead of being subject to the impulse of various and particular desires, they, with one fixed and immoveable will, long for the kingdom of God, which consists not less in the destruction of the ungodly than in the salvation of believers. If this be so, there cannot be a doubt that their charity is confined to the communion of Christ's body, and extends no farther than is compatible with the nature of that communion.

But though I grant that in this way they pray for us, they do not, however, lose their quiescence so as to be distracted with earthly cares: far less are they, therefore, to be invoked by us. Nor does it follow that such invocation is to be used because, while men are alive upon the earth, they can mutually commend themselves to each other's prayers. It serves to keep alive a feeling of charity when they, as it were, share each other's wants, and bear each other's burdens. This they do by the command of the Lord, and not without a promise, the two things of primary importance in prayer. But all such reasons are inapplicable to the dead, with whom the Lord, in withdrawing them from our society, has left us no means of intercourse (Ecclesiastes 9:5, 6), and to whom, so far as we can conjecture, he has left no means of intercourse with us. But if any one allege that they certainly must retain the same charity for us, as they are united with us in one faith, who has revealed to us that they have ears capable of listening to the sounds of our voice, or eyes clear enough to discern our necessities?

Our opponents, indeed, talk in the shade of their schools of some kind of light which beams upon departed saints from the divine countenance, and in which, as in a mirror, they, from their lofty abode, behold the affairs of men; but to affirm this with the confidence which these men presume to use, is just to desire, by means of the extravagant dreams of our own brain, and without any authority, to pry and penetrate into the hidden judgments of God, and trample upon Scripture, which so often declares that the wisdom of our flesh is at enmity with the wisdom of God, utterly condemns the vanity of our mind, and humbling our reason, bids us look only to the will of God.

CHAPTER 25

• A refutation of one further argument founded on a passage in Moses.

The other passages of Scripture which they employ to defend their error are miserably wrested. Jacob (they say) asks for the sons of Joseph, "Let my name be named on them, and the name of my fathers, Abraham and Isaac" (Genesis 48:16). First, let us see what the nature of this invocation was among the Israelites. They do not implore their fathers to bring succor to them, but they beseech God to remember his servants, Abraham, Isaac, and Jacob. Their example, therefore, gives no countenance to those who use addresses to the saints themselves.

But such being the dullness of these blocks, that they comprehend not what it is to invoke the name of Jacob, nor why it is to be invoked, it is not strange that they blunder thus childishly as to the mode of doing it. The expression repeatedly occurs in Scripture. Isaiah speaks of women being called by the name of men, when they have them for husbands and live under their protection (Isaiah 4:1). The calling of the name of Abraham over the Israelites consists in referring the origin of their race to him, and holding him in distinguished remembrance as their author and parent. Jacob does not do so from any anxiety to extend the celebrity of his name, but because he knows that all the happiness of his posterity consisted in the inheritance of the covenant which God had made with them. Seeing that this would give them the sum of all blessings, he prays that they may be regarded as of his race, this being nothing else than to transmit the succession of the covenant to them.

They again, when they make mention of this subject in their prayers, do not betake themselves to the intercession of the dead, but call to remembrance that covenant in which their most merciful Father undertakes to be kind and propitious to them for the sake of Abraham, Isaac, and Jacob. How little, in other respects, the saints trusted to the merits of their fathers, the public voice of the Church declares in the prophets "Doubtless thou art our Father, though Abraham be ignorant of us, and Israel acknowledge us not; thou, O Lord, art our Father, our Redeemer" (Isaiah 63:16). And while the Church thus speaks, she at the same time adds, "Return for thy servants' sake," not thinking of anything like intercession, but adverting only to the benefit of the covenant. Now, indeed, when we have the Lord Jesus, in whose hand the eternal covenant of mercy was not only made but confirmed, what better name can we bear before us in our prayers? And since those good Doctors would make out by these words that the Patriarchs are intercessors, I should like them to tell me why, in so great a multitude[12], no place whatever is given to Abraham, the father of the Church? We know well from what a crew they select their intercessors[13]. Let them then tell me what consistency there is in neglecting and rejecting Abraham, whom God preferred to all others, and raised to the highest degree of honor.

The only reason is, that as it was plain there was no such practice in the ancient Church, they thought proper to conceal the novelty of the practice by saying nothing of the Patriarchs: as if by a mere diversity of names they could excuse a practice at once novel and impure. They sometimes, also, object that God is entreated to have mercy on his people "for David's sake" (Psalm 132:10; see *Calvin's Commentaries.*). This is so far from supporting their error, that it is the strongest refutation of it. We must consider the character which David bore. He is set apart from the whole body of the faithful to establish the covenant which God made in his hand. Thus regard is had to the covenant rather than to the individual. Under him as a type the sole intercession of Christ is asserted. But what was peculiar to David as a type of Christ is certainly inapplicable to others.

---

[12] The French adds, "et quasi en une fourmiliere de saincts;"--and as it were a swarm of saints.

[13] French, "C'est chose trop notoire de quel bourbieu ou de quelle racaille ils tirent leur saincts."--It is too notorious out of what mire or rubbish they draw their saints.

CHAPTER 26

• *A refutation of one more argument from its being said that
the prayers of saints are heard.*

But some seem to be moved by the fact, that the prayers of saints
are often said to have been heard. Why? Because they prayed. "They
cried unto thee" (says the Psalmist), "and were delivered: they trusted
in thee, and were not confounded" (Psalm 22:5). Let us also pray after
their example, that like them we too may be heard. Those men, on the
contrary, absurdly argue that none will be heard but those who have
been heard already.

How much better does James argue, "Elias was a man subject to
like passions as we are, and he prayed earnestly that it might not
rain: and it rained not on the earth by the space of three years and
six months. And he prayed again and the heaven gave rain, and the
earth brought forth her fruit" (James 5:17, 18). What? Does he
infer that Elias possessed some peculiar privilege, and that we must
have recourse to him for the use of it? By no means. He shows the
perpetual efficacy of a pure and pious prayer, that we may be induced
in like manner to pray. For the kindness and readiness of God to hear
others is malignantly interpreted, if their example does not inspire
us with stronger confidence in his promise, since his declaration is
not that he will incline his ear to one or two, or a few individuals,
but to all who call upon his name. In this ignorance they are the
less excusable, because they seem as it were avowedly to contemn the
many admonitions of Scripture.

David was repeatedly delivered by the power of God. Was this to give
that power to him that we might be delivered on his application? Very
different is his affirmation: "The righteous shall compass me about;
for thou shalt deal bountifully with me" (Psalm 142:7). Again, "The
righteous also shall see, and fear, and shall laugh at him" (Psalm 52:6).
"This poor man cried, and the Lord heard him, and saved him out of all

his troubles" (Psalm 34:6). In The Psalms are many similar prayers, in which David calls upon God to give him what he asks, for this reason, viz., that the righteous may not be put to shame, but by his example encouraged to hope. Here let one passage suffice, "For this shall every one that is godly pray unto thee in a time when thou mayest be found" (Psalm 32:6, Calvin's Commentaries). This passage I have quoted the more readily, because those ravers who employ their hireling tongues in defense of the Papacy, are not ashamed to adduce it in proof of the intercession of the dead. As if David intended anything more than to show the benefit which he shall obtain from the divine clemency and condescension when he shall have been heard. In general, we must hold that the experience of the grace of God, as well towards ourselves as towards others, tends in no slight degree to confirm our faith in his promises. I do not quote the many passages in which David sets forth the loving-kindness of God to him as a ground of confidence, as they will readily occur to every reader of The Psalms.

Jacob had previously taught the same thing by his own example, "I am not worthy of the least of all thy mercies, and of all the truth which thou hast showed unto thy servant: for with my staff I passed over this Jordan; and now I am become two bands" (Genesis 32:10). He indeed alleges the promise, but not the promise only; for he at the same time adds the effect, to animate him with greater confidence in the future kindness of God. God is not like men who grow weary of their liberality, or whose means of exercising it become exhausted; but he is to be estimated by his own nature, as David properly does when he says, "Thou hast redeemed me, O Lord God of truth" (Psalm 31:5). After ascribing the praise of his salvation to God, he adds that he is true: for were he not ever like himself, his past favor would not be an infallible ground for confidence and prayer.

But when we know that as often as he assists us, he gives us a specimen and proof of his goodness and faithfulness, there is no reason to fear that our hope will be ashamed or frustrated.

CHAPTER 27

- *Saints cannot be invoked without impiety.*

    a. It robs God of his glory.

    b. It destroys the intercession of Christ.

    c. It is repugnant to the word of God.

    d. It is opposed to the true method of prayer.

    e. It is without approved example.

    f. It springs from distrust.

On the whole, since Scripture places the principal part of worship in the invocation of God (this being the office of piety which he requires of us in preference to all sacrifices), it is manifest sacrilege to offer prayer to others. Hence it is said in the psalm: "If we have forgotten the name of our God, or stretched out our hands to a strange god, shall not God search this out?" (Psalm 44:20, 21). Again, since it is only in faith that God desires to be invoked, and he distinctly enjoins us to frame our prayers according to the rule of his word: in fine, since faith is founded on the word, and is the parent of right prayer, the moment we decline from the word, our prayers are impure. But we have already shown, that if we consult the whole volume of Scripture, we shall find that God claims this honor to himself alone. In regard to the office of intercession, we have also seen that it is peculiar to Christ, and that no prayer is agreeable to God which he as Mediator does not sanctify.

And though believers mutually offer up prayers to God in behalf of their brethren, we have shown that this derogates in no respect from the sole intercession of Christ, because all trust to that intercession in commending themselves as well as others to God. Moreover, we have shown that this is ignorantly transferred to the dead, of whom we nowhere read that they were commanded to pray for us. The Scripture often exhorts us to offer up mutual prayers; but says not one syllable concerning the dead; nay, James tacitly excludes the dead when he combines the two things, to "confess our sins one to another, and to pray one for another" (James 5:16). Hence it is sufficient to condemn this error, that the beginning of right prayer springs from faith, and that faith comes by the hearing of the word of God, in which there is no mention of fictitious intercession, superstition having rashly adopted intercessors who have not been divinely appointed.

While the Scripture abounds in various forms of prayer, we find no example of this intercession, without which Papists think there is no prayer. Moreover, it is evident that this superstition is the result of distrust, because they are either not contented with Christ as an intercessor, or have altogether robbed him of this honor. This last is easily proved by their effrontery in maintaining, as the strongest of all their arguments for the intercession of the saints, that we are unworthy of familiar access to God. This, indeed, we acknowledge to be most true, but we thence infer that they leave nothing to Christ, because they consider his intercession as nothing, unless it is supplemented by that of George and Hypolyte, and similar phantoms.

CHAPTER 28

- *Different kinds of prayer: vows, supplications, petitions, thanksgiving. How they are connected, implemented and why.*

- *Explanation of prayer confirmed by reason, Scripture, and example.*

But though prayer is properly confined to vows and supplications, yet so strong is the affinity between petition and thanksgiving, that both may be conveniently comprehended under one name. For the forms which Paul enumerates (1 Timothy 2:1) fall under the first member of this division. By prayer and supplication we pour out our desires before God, asking as well those things which tend to promote his glory and display his name, as the benefits which contribute to our advantage. By thanksgiving we duly celebrate his kindnesses toward us, ascribing to his liberality every blessing which enters into our lot. David accordingly includes both in one sentence, "Call upon me in the day of trouble: I will deliver thee, and thou shalt glorify me" (Psalm 50:15). Scripture, not without reason, commands us to use both continually.

We have already described the greatness of our want, while experience itself proclaims the straits which press us on every side to be so numerous and so great, that all have sufficient ground to send forth sighs and groans to God without intermission, and suppliantly implore him. For even should they be exempt from adversity, still the holiest ought to be stimulated first by their sins, and, secondly, by the innumerable assaults of temptation, to long for a remedy. The sacrifice of praise and thanksgiving can never be interrupted without guilt, since God never ceases to load us with favor upon favor, so as to force us to gratitude, however slow and sluggish we may be. In short, so great and widely diffused are the riches of his liberality towards us, so marvelous and wondrous the miracles which we behold on every side, that we never can want a subject and materials for praise and thanksgiving.

To make this somewhat clearer: since all our hopes and resources are placed in God (this has already been fully proved), so that neither our persons nor our interests can prosper without his blessing, we must constantly submit ourselves and our all to him. Then whatever we deliberate, speak, or do, should be deliberated, spoken, and done under his hand and will; in fine, under the hope of his assistance. God has pronounced a curse upon all who, confiding in themselves or others, form plans and resolutions, who, without regarding his will, or invoking his aid, either plan or attempt to execute (James 4:14; Isaiah 30:1; Isaiah 31:1).

And since, as has already been observed, he receives the honor which is due when he is acknowledged to be the author of all good, it follows that, in deriving all good from his hand, we ought continually to express our thankfulness, and that we have no right to use the benefits which proceed from his liberality, if we do not assiduously proclaim his praise, and give him thanks, these being the ends for which they are given. When Paul declares that every creature of God "is sanctified by the word of God and prayers" (1 Timothy 4:5), he intimates that without the word and prayers none of them are holy and pure, word being used metonymically for faith. Hence David, on experiencing the loving-kindness of the Lord, elegantly declares, "He hath put a new song in my mouth" (Psalm 40:3); intimating, that our silence is malignant when we leave his blessings unpraised, seeing every blessing he bestows is a new ground of thanksgiving. Thus Isaiah, proclaiming the singular mercies of God, says, "Sing unto the Lord a new song" (Isaiah 42:10). In the same sense David says in another passage, "O Lord, open thou my lips; and my mouth shall show forth thy praise" (Psalm 41:15). In like manner, Hezekiah and Jonah declare that they will regard it as the end of their deliverance "to celebrate the goodness of God with songs in his temple" (Isaiah 38:20; Jonah 2:10). David lays down a general rule for all believers in these words, "What shall I render unto the Lord for all his benefits toward me? I will take the cup of salvation, and call upon the name of the Lord" (Psalm 116:12, 13). This rule the Church follows in another psalm, "Save us, O Lord our God, and gather us from among the heathen, to give thanks unto thy holy name, and to triumph in thy praise" (Psalm 106:47). Again, " He will regard the prayer of the destitute, and not despise their prayer. This shall be written for the generation to come: and the people which shall be created shall praise the Lord." "To declare the name of the Lord in Zion, and his praise in Jerusalem" (Psalm 102:18, 21). Nay, whenever believers beseech the Lord to do anything for his own name's sake, as they declare themselves unworthy of obtaining it in their own name, so they oblige themselves to give thanks, and promise to make the right use of his loving-kindness by being the heralds of it.

Thus Hosea, speaking of the future redemption of the Church, says, "Take away all iniquity, and receive us graciously; so will we render the calves of our lips" (Hosea 14:2). Not only do our tongues proclaim the kindness of God, but they naturally inspire us with love to him. "I love the Lord, because he hath heard my voice and my supplications" (Psalm 116:1). In another passage, speaking of the help which he had experienced, he says, "I will love thee, O Lord, my strength" (Psalm 18:1). No praise will ever please God that does not flow from this feeling of love. Nay, we must attend to the declaration of Paul, that all wishes are vicious and perverse which are not accompanied with thanksgiving. His words are, "In everything by prayer and supplication with thanksgiving let your requests be made known unto God" (Philippians 4:6). Because many, under the influence of moroseness, weariness, impatience, bitter grief and fear, use murmuring in their prayers, he enjoins us so to regulate our feelings as cheerfully to bless God even before obtaining what we ask.

But if this connection ought always to subsist in full vigor between things that are almost contrary, the more sacred is the tie which binds us to celebrate the praises of God whenever he grants our requests. And as we have already shown that our prayers, which otherwise would be polluted, are sanctified by the intercession of Christ, so the Apostle, by enjoining us "to offer the sacrifice of praise to God continually" by

Christ (Hebrews 13:15), reminds us, that without the intervention of his priesthood our lips are not pure enough to celebrate the name of God. Hence we infer that a monstrous delusion prevails among Papists, the great majority of whom wonder when Christ is called an intercessor. The reason why Paul enjoins, "Pray without ceasing; in everything give thanks" (1 Thessalonians 5:17, 18), is, because he would have us with the utmost assiduity, at all times, in every place, in all things, and under all circumstances, direct our prayers to God, to expect all the things which we desire from him, and when obtained ascribe them to him; thus furnishing perpetual grounds for prayer and praise.

CHAPTER 29

- *he facets of prayer, viz., private and public, constant, at stated seasons, etc.*

- *The nature of prayer without ceasing.*

- *The garrulity of Papists and hypocrites refuted.*

- *The scope and parts of prayer.*

- *Secret prayer.*

- *Prayer in all places.*

This assiduity in prayer, though it specially refers to the peculiar private prayers of individuals, extends also in some measure to the public prayers of the Church. These, it may be said, cannot be continual, and ought not to be made, except in the manner which, for the sake of order, has been established by public consent. This I admit, and hence certain hours are fixed beforehand, hours which, though indifferent in regard to God, are necessary for the use of man, that the general convenience may be consulted, and all things be done in the Church, as Paul enjoins, "decently and in order" (1 Corinthians 14:40). But there is nothing in this to prevent each church from being now and then stirred up to a more frequent use of prayer and being more zealously affected under the impulse of some greater necessity. Of perseverance in prayer, which is much akin to assiduity, we shall speak towards the close of the chapter (chapter 51, 52). This assiduity, moreover, is very different from the BATTOLOGIAN (Greek -- English "yammering"), vain speaking, which our Savior has prohibited (Matthew 6:7). For he does not there forbid us to pray long or frequently, or with great fervor, but warns us against supposing that we can extort anything from God by importuning him with garrulous loquacity, as if he were to be persuaded after the manner of men.

We know that hypocrites, because they consider not that they have to do with God, offer up their prayers as pompously as if it were part of a triumphal show. The Pharisee, who thanked God that he was not as other men, no doubt proclaimed his praises before men, as if he had wished to gain a reputation for sanctity by his prayers. Hence that vain speaking, which for a similar reason prevails so much in the Papacy in the present day, some vainly spinning out the time by a reiteration of the same frivolous prayers, and others employing a long series of verbiage for vulgar display[14]. This childish garrulity being a mockery of God, it is not strange that it is prohibited in the Church, in order that every feeling there expressed may be sincere, proceeding from the inmost heart. Akin to this abuse is another which our Savior also condemns, namely, when hypocrites for the sake of ostentation court the presence of many witnesses, and would sooner pray in the market-place than pray without applause. The true object of prayer being, as we have already said (sec. 4, 5), to carry our thoughts directly to God, whether to celebrate his praise or implore his aid, we can easily see that its primary seat is in the mind and heart, or rather that prayer itself is properly an effusion and manifestation of internal feeling before Him who is the searcher of hearts.

Hence (as has been said), when our divine Master was pleased to lay down the best rule for prayer, his injunction was, "Enter into thy closet, and when thou hast shut thy door, pray to thy Father which is in secret, and thy Father which seeth in secret shall reward thee openly"

---

[14] French, "Cette longueur de priere a aujourd'hui sa vogue en la Papauté, et procede de cette mesme source; c'est que les uns barbotant force Ave Maria, et reiterant cent fois un chapelet, perdent une partie du temps; les autres, comme les chanoines et caphars, en abayant le parchemin jour et nuict, et barbotant leur breviaire vendent leur coquilles au peuple."--This long prayer is at present in vogue among the Papists, and proceeds from the same cause: some muttering a host of Hail Mary's, and going over their beads a hundred times, lose part of their time; others, as the canons and monks grumbling over their parchment night and day, and muttering their breviary, sell their cockleshells to the people.

(Matthew 6:6). Dissuading us from the example of hypocrites, who sought the applause of men by an ambitious ostentation in prayer, he adds the better course -- enter thy chamber, shut thy door, and there pray. By these words (as I understand them) he taught us to seek a place of retirement which might enable us to turn all our thoughts inwards and enter deeply into our hearts, promising that God would hold converse with the feelings of our mind, of which the body ought to be the temple. He meant not to deny that it may be expedient to pray in other places also, but he shows that prayer is somewhat of a secret nature, having its chief seat in the mind, and requiring a tranquility far removed from the turmoil of ordinary cares.

And hence it was not without cause that our Lord himself, when he would engage more earnestly in prayer, withdrew into a retired spot beyond the bustle of the world, thus reminding us by his example that we are not to neglect those helps which enable the mind, in itself too much disposed to wander, to become sincerely intent on prayer. Meanwhile, as he abstained not from prayer when the occasion required it, though he were in the midst of a crowd, so must we, whenever there is need, lift up "pure hands" (1 Timothy 2:8) at all places. And hence we must hold that he who declines to pray in the public meeting of the saints, knows not what it is to pray apart, in retirement, or at home.

On the other hand, he who neglects to pray alone and in private, however sedulously he frequents public meetings, there gives his prayers to the wind, because he defers more to the opinion of man than to the secret judgment of God. Still, lest the public prayers of the Church should be held in contempt, the Lord anciently bestowed upon them the most honorable appellation, especially when he called the temple the "house of prayer" (Isaiah 56:7). For by this expression he both showed that the duty of prayer is a principal part of his worship, and that to enable believers to engage in it with one consent his temple is set up before them as a kind of banner. A noble promise was also added, "Praise waiteth for thee, O God, in Zion: and unto thee shall the vow be performed[15]" (Psalm 65:1). By these words the Psalmist reminds us that the prayers of the Church are never in vain; because God always furnishes his people with materials for a song of joy.

But although the shadows of the law have ceased, yet because God was pleased by this ordinance to foster the unity of the faith among us also, there can be no doubt that the same promise belongs to us -- a promise which Christ sanctioned with his own lips, and which Paul declares to be perpetually in force.

---

[15] Calvin translates, "Te expectat Deus, laus in Sion,"--God, the praise in Zion waiteth for thee.

CHAPTER 30

- *Public places or churches in which common prayers are offered up.*

- *Proper use of churches.*

As God in his word enjoins common prayer, so public temples are the places destined for the performance of them, and hence those who refuse to join with the people of God in this observance have no ground for the pretext, that they enter their chamber in order that they may obey the command of the Lord. For he who promises to grant whatsoever two or three assembled in his name shall ask (Matthew 18:20), declares, that he by no means despises the prayers which are publicly offered up, provided there be no ostentation, or catching at human applause, and provided there be a true and sincere affection in the secret recesses of the heart[16].

If this is the legitimate use of churches (and it certainly is), we must, on the other hand, beware of imitating the practice which commenced some centuries ago, of imagining that churches are the proper dwellings of God, where he is more ready to listen to us, or of attaching to them some kind of secret sanctity, which makes prayer there more holy. For seeing we are the true temples of God, we must pray in ourselves if we would invoke God in his holy temple. Let us leave such gross ideas to the Jews or the heathen, knowing that we have a command to pray without distinction of place, "in spirit and in truth" (John 4:23). It is true that by the order of God the temple was anciently dedicated for the offering of prayers and sacrifices, but this was at a time when the truth (which being now fully manifested,

---

[16] See Book I. chap. xi. sec. 7,13, on the subject of images in churches. Also Book IV. chap. iv. sec. 8, and chap. v. sec. 18, as to the ornaments of churches.

we are not permitted to confine to any material temple) lay hid under the figure of shadows.

Even the temple was not represented to the Jews as confining the presence of God within its walls, but was meant to train them to contemplate the image of the true temple. Accordingly, a severe rebuke is administered both by Isaiah and Stephen, to those who thought that God could in any way dwell in temples made with hands (Isaiah 66:2; Acts 7:48).

CHAPTER 31

- *Of utterance and singing: These are of no avail if not from the heart.*

- *The use of the voice refers more to public than private prayer.*

Hence it is perfectly clear that neither words nor singing (if used in prayer) are of the least consequence, or avail one iota with God, unless they proceed from deep feeling in the heart. Nay, rather they provoke his anger against us, if they come from the lips and throat only, since this is to abuse his sacred name, and hold his majesty in derision. This we infer from the words of Isaiah, which, though their meaning is of wider extent, go to rebuke this vice also: "Forasmuch as this people draw near me with their mouth, and with their lips do honor me, but have removed their heart far from me, and their fear toward me is taught by the precept of men: therefore, behold, I will proceed to do a marvelous work among this people, even a marvelous work and a wonder: for the wisdom of their wise men shall perish, and the understanding of their prudent men shall be hid" (Isaiah 29:13).

Still we do not condemn words or singing, but rather greatly commend them, provided the feeling of the mind goes along with them. For in this way the thought of God is kept alive on our minds, which, from their fickle and versatile nature, soon relax, and are distracted by various objects, unless various means are used to support them. Besides, since the glory of God ought in a manner to be displayed in each part of our body, the special service to which the tongue should be devoted is that of singing and speaking, inasmuch as it has been expressly created to declare and proclaim the praise of God.

This employment of the tongue is chiefly in the public services which are performed in the meeting of the saints. In this way the God whom we serve in one spirit and one faith, we glorify together as it were with one voice and one mouth; and that openly, so that each may in turn receive the confession of his brother's faith, and be invited and incited to imitate it.

CHAPTER 32

- *Singing is from the oldest antiquity, although it is not universal.*

- *How singing is to be performed.*

It is certain that the use of singing in churches (which I may mention in passing) is not only very ancient, but was also used by the Apostles, as we may gather from the words of Paul, "I will sing with the spirit, and I will sing with the understanding also" (1 Corinthians 14:15). In like manner he says to the Colossians, "Teaching and admonishing one another in psalms, and hymns, and spiritual songs, singing with grace in your hearts to the Lord" (Colossians 3:16). In the former passage, he enjoins us to sing with the voice and the heart; in the latter, he commends spiritual Songs, by which the pious mutually edify each other.

That it was not an universal practice, however, is attested by Augustine (*Confessions*, book 9, chapter 7), who states that the church of Milan first began to use singing in the time of Ambrose, when the orthodox faith being persecuted by Justina, the mother of Valentinian, the vigils of the people were more frequent than usual[17]; and that the practice was afterwards followed by the other Western churches. He had said a little before that the custom came from the East[18]. He also intimates (*Retract* book 2). that it was received in Africa in his own time. His words are, "Hilarius, a man of tribunitial rank, assailed with the bitterest invectives he could use the custom which then began to exist at Carthage, of singing hymns from the book of Psalms at the

---

[17] This clause of the sentence is omitted in the French.

[18] The French adds, "où on en avoit tousjours usé;"--where it had always been used.

altar, either before the oblation, or when it was distributed to the people; I answered him, at the request of my brethren[19]."

And certainly if singing is tempered to a gravity befitting the presence of God and angels, it both gives dignity and grace to sacred actions, and has a very powerful tendency to stir up the mind to true zeal and ardor in prayer. We must, however, carefully beware, lest our ears be more intent on the music than our minds on the spiritual meaning of the words. Augustine confesses (*Confessions*, book 10, chapter 33) that the fear of this danger sometimes made him wish for the introduction of a practice observed by Athanasius, who ordered the reader to use only a gentle inflection of the voice, more akin to recitation than singing. But on again considering how many advantages were derived from singing, he inclined to the other side[20]. If this moderation is used, there cannot be a doubt that the practice is most sacred and salutary.

On the other hand, songs composed merely to tickle and delight the ear are unbecoming the majesty of the Church, and cannot but be most displeasing to God.

---

[19] The whole of this quotation is omitted in the French

[20] French, "Mais il adjouste d'autre part, que quand il se souvenoit du fruict et de l'edification qu'il avoit recue en oyant chanter àl'Eglise il enclinoit plus à l'autre partie, c'est, approuver le chant;"--but he adds on the other hand that when he called to mind the fruit and edification which he had received from hearing singing in the church, he inclined more to the other side; that is, to approve singing.

CHAPTER 33

- *Two reasons public prayers should be in the vernacular, not in a foreign tongue.*

  a. The nature of the Church.

  b. Authority of an apostle.

- *Sincere affection is always necessary, but the tongue is not always necessary.*

- *Postures of prayer: Bending the knee, and uncovering the head.*

It is also plain that the public prayers are not to be couched in Greek among the Latins, nor in Latin among the French or English (as hitherto has been everywhere practiced), but in the vulgar tongue, so that all present may understand them, since they ought to be used for the edification of the whole Church, which cannot be in the least degree benefited by a sound not understood.

Those who are not moved by any reason of humanity or charity, ought at least to be somewhat moved by the authority of Paul, whose words are by no means ambiguous: "When thou shalt bless with the spirit, how shall he that occupieth the room of the unlearned say, Amen, at thy giving of thanks, seeing he understandeth not what thou sayest? For thou verily givest thanks, but the other is not edified" (1 Corinthians 14:16, 17). How then can one sufficiently admire the unbridled license of the Papists, who, while the Apostle publicly protests against it, hesitate not to bawl out the most verbose prayers in a foreign tongue, prayers of which they themselves sometimes do not understand one syllable, and which they have no wish that others should understand[21]? Different is the course which Paul prescribes,

---

[21] French, "Qui est-ce donc qui se pourra assez esmerveiller d'une audace tant

"What is it then? I will pray with the spirit, and I will pray with the understanding also; I will sing with the spirit, and I will sing with the understanding also:" meaning by the spirit the special gift of tongues, which some who had received it abused when they dissevered it from the mind, that is, the understanding. The principle we must always hold is, that in all prayer, public and private, the tongue without the mind must be displeasing to God. Moreover, the mind must be so incited, as in ardor of thought far to surpass what the tongue is able to express.

Lastly, the tongue is not even necessary to private prayer, unless in so far as the internal feeling is insufficient for incitement, or the vehemence of the incitement carries the utterance of the tongue along with it. For although the best prayers are sometimes without utterance, yet when the feeling of the mind is overpowering, the tongue spontaneously breaks forth into utterance, and our other members into gesture. Hence that dubious muttering of Hannah (1 Samuel 1:13), something similar to which is experienced by all the saints when concise and abrupt expressions escape from them.

The bodily gestures usually observed in prayer, such as kneeling and uncovering of the head (Acts 20:36), are exercises by which we attempt to rise to higher veneration of God.

---

effrenee qu'ont eu les Papistes et ont encore, qui contre la defense de l'Apostre, chantent et brayent de langue estrange et inconnue, en laquelle le plus souvent ils n'entendent pas eux mesmes une syllabe, et ne veulent que les autres y entendent?"--Who then can sufficiently admire the unbridled audacity which the Papists have had, and still have, who, contrary to the prohibition of the Apostle, chant and bray in a foreign and unknown tongue, in which, for the most part, they do not understand one syllable, and which they have no wish that others understand?

CHAPTER 34

- *The form of prayer delivered by Christ displays the boundless goodness of our heavenly Father.*

- *The great comfort this affords.*

We must now attend not only to a surer method, but also form of prayer, that, namely, which our heavenly Father has delivered to us by his beloved Son, and in which we may recognize his boundless goodness and condescension (Matthew 6:9; Luke 11:2). Besides admonishing and exhorting us to seek him in our every necessity (as children are wont to betake themselves to the protection of their parents when oppressed with any anxiety), seeing that we were not fully aware how great our poverty was, or what was right or for our interest to ask, he has provided for this ignorance; that wherein our capacity failed he has sufficiently supplied. For he has given us a form in which is set before us as in a picture everything which it is lawful to wish, everything which is conducive to our interest, everything which it is necessary to demand. From his goodness in this respect we derive the great comfort of knowing, that as we ask almost in his words, we ask nothing that is absurd, or foreign, or unseasonable; nothing, in short, that is not agreeable to him.

Plato, seeing the ignorance of men in presenting their desires to God, desires which if granted would often be most injurious to them, declares the best form of prayer to be that which an ancient poet has furnished: "O king Jupiter, give what is best, whether we wish it or wish it not; but avert from us what is evil even though we ask it" (Plato, *Alcibiad* ii). This heathen shows his wisdom in discerning how dangerous it is to ask of God what our own passion dictates; while, at the same time, he reminds us of our unhappy condition in not being able to open our lips before God without dangers unless his Spirit instruct us how to pray aright (Romans 8:26). The higher value, therefore, ought we to set on the privilege, when the only begotten Son of God puts words into our lips, and thus relieves our minds of all hesitation.

CHAPTER 35

- *The Lord's Prayer is divided into six petitions.*

- *It is further subdivided into two principal parts, the former referring to the glory of God, the latter to our salvation*

This form or rule of prayer is composed of six petitions. For I am prevented from agreeing with those who divide it into seven by the adversative mode of diction used by the Evangelist, who appears to have intended to unite the two members together; as if he had said, Do not allow us to be overcome by temptation, but rather bring assistance to our frailty, and deliver us that we may not fall. Ancient writers[22] also agree with us, that what is added by Matthew as a seventh head is to be considered as explanatory of the sixth petition[23]. But though in every part of the prayer the first place is assigned to the glory of God, still this is more especially the object of the three first petitions, in which we are to look to the glory of God alone, without any reference to what is called our own advantage. The three remaining petitions are devoted to our interest, and properly relate to things which it is useful for us to ask. When we ask that the name of God may be hallowed, as God wishes to prove whether we love and serve him freely, or from the hope of reward, we are not to think at all of our own interest; we must set his glory before our eyes, and keep them intent upon it alone. In the other similar petitions, this is the only manner in which we ought

---

[22] Augustine in *Enchiridion ad Laurent.* xxx. 116. Pseudo-Chrysost. in *Homilies on Matthew*, hom. xiv.

[23] Dont il est facile de juger que ce qui est adjousté en S. Matthieu, et qu'aucuns ont pris pour une septieme requeste, n'est qu'un explication de la sixieme, et se doit a icelle rapporter;"--Whence it is easy to perceive that what is added in St. Matthew, and which some have taken for a seventh petition, is only an explanation of the sixth, and ought to be referred to it.

to be affected. It is true, that in this way our own interest is greatly promoted, because, when the name of God is hallowed in the way we ask, our own sanctification also is thereby promoted.

But in regard to this advantage, we must, as I have said, shut our eyes, and be in a manner blind, so as not even to see it; and hence were all hope of our private advantage cut off, we still should never cease to wish and pray for this hallowing, and everything else which pertains to the glory of God. We have examples in Moses and Paul, who did not count it grievous to turn away their eyes and minds from themselves, and with intense and fervent zeal long for death, if by their loss the kingdom and glory of God might be promoted (Exodus 32:32; Romans 9:3).

On the other hand, when we ask for daily bread, although we desire what is advantageous for ourselves, we ought also especially to seek the glory of God, so much so that we would not ask at all unless it were to turn to his glory. Let us now proceed to an exposition of the Prayer. OUR FATHER WHICH ART IN HEAVEN.

CHAPTER 36

- *The use of the term "Father" implies:*

    a. That we pray to God in the name of Christ alone.

    b. That we lay aside all distrust.

    c. That we expect everything that is for our good.

The first thing suggested at the very outset is, as we have already said (chapters 17-19), that all our prayers to God ought only to be presented in the name of Christ, as there is no other name which can recommend them. In calling God our Father, we certainly plead the name of Christ. For with what confidence could any man call God his Father? Who would have the presumption to arrogate to himself the honor of a son of God were we not gratuitously adopted as his sons in Christ? He being the true Son, has been given to us as a brother, so that that which he possesses as his own by nature becomes ours by adoption, if we embrace this great mercy with firm faith. As John says, "As many as received him, to them gave he power to become the sons of God, even to them that believe in his name" (John 1:12).

Hence he both calls himself our Father, and is pleased to be so called by us, by this delightful name relieving us of all distrust, since nowhere can a stronger affection be found than in a father. Hence, too, he could not have given us a stronger testimony of his boundless love than in calling us his sons. But his love towards us is so much the greater and more excellent than that of earthly parents, the farther he surpasses all men in goodness and mercy (Isaiah 63:16). Earthly parents, laying aside all paternal affection, might abandon their offspring; he will never abandon us (Psalm 27:10), seeing he cannot deny himself. For we have his promise, "If ye then, being evil, know how to give good gifts unto your children, how much more shall your Father which is in heaven give good things to them that ask him?" (Matthew 7:11). In like manner in the prophet, "Can a woman forget her sucking child, that she should not have compassion on the son of her womb? Yea, they may forget, yet will not I forget thee" (Isaiah 49:15).

But if we are his sons, then as a son cannot betake himself to the protection of a stranger and a foreigner without at the same time complaining of his father's cruelty or poverty, so we cannot ask assistance from any other quarter than from him, unless we would upbraid him with poverty, or want of means, or cruelty and excessive austerity.

CHAPTER 37

- *Don't our sins exclude us from the presence of him whom we have made a Judge, not a Father? A response from the nature of God, the parable of the prodigal son, and from the expression, "Our Father."*

- *Christ is the earnest and the Holy Spirit the witness of our adoption.*

Nor let us allege that we are justly rendered timid by a consciousness of sin, by which our Father, though mild and merciful, is daily offended. For if among men a son cannot have a better advocate to plead his cause with his father, and cannot employ a better intercessor to regain his lost favor, than if he come himself suppliant and downcast, acknowledging his fault, to implore the mercy of his father, whose paternal feelings cannot but be moved by such entreaties, what will that "Father of all mercies, and God of all comfort," do? (2 Corinthians 1:3). Will he not rather listen to the tears and groans of his children, when supplicating for themselves (especially seeing he invites and exhorts us to do so), than to any advocacy of others to whom the timid have recourse, not without some semblance of despair, because they are distrustful of their father's mildness and clemency? The exuberance of his paternal kindness he sets before us in the parable (Luke 15:20). when the father with open arms receives the son who had gone away from him, wasted his substance in riotous living, and in all ways grievously sinned against him. He waits not till pardon is asked in words, but, anticipating the request, recognizes him afar off, runs to meet him, consoles him, and restores him to favor.

By setting before us this admirable example of mildness in a man, he designed to show in how much greater abundance we may expect it from him who is not only a Father, but the best and most merciful of all fathers, however ungrateful, rebellious, and wicked sons we may be, provided only we throw ourselves upon his mercy. And the better to assure us that he is such a Father if we are Christians, he has been pleased to be called not only a Father, but our Father, as if we were pleading with him after this manner, O Father, who art possessed of so much affection for thy children, and art so ready to forgive, we thy children approach thee and present our requests, fully persuaded that thou hast no other feelings towards us than those of a father, though we are unworthy of such a parent[24].

But as our narrow hearts are incapable of comprehending such boundless favor, Christ is not only the earnest and pledge of our adoption, but also gives us the Spirit as a witness of this adoption, that through him we may freely cry aloud, Abba, Father. Whenever, therefore, we are restrained by any feeling of hesitation, let us remember to ask of him that he may correct our timidity, and placing us under the magnanimous guidance of the Spirit, enable us to pray boldly.

---

[24] French, "Quelque mauvaistié qu'ayons euë, ou quelque imperfection ou poureté qui soit en nous;"--whatever wickedness we may have done, or whatever imperfection or poverty there may be in us.

CHAPTER 38

• Why God is generally called "Our Father".

The instruction given us, however, is not that every individual in particular is to call him Father, but rather that we are all in common to call him Our Father. By this we are reminded how strong the feeling of brotherly love between us ought to be, since we are all alike, by the same mercy and free kindness, the children of such a Father. For if He from whom we all obtain whatever is good is our common Father (Matthew 23:9), everything which has been distributed to us we should be prepared to communicate to each other, as far as occasion demands. But if we are thus desirous as we ought, to stretch out our hands and give assistance to each other, there is nothing by which we can more benefit our brethren than by committing them to the care and protection of the best of parents, since if He is propitious and favorable nothing more can be desired. And, indeed, we owe this also to our Father. For as he who truly and from the heart loves the father of a family, extends the same love and good-will to all his household, so the zeal and affection which we feel for our heavenly Parent it becomes us to extend towards his people, his family, and, in fine, his heritage, which he has honored so highly as to give them the appellation of the " fullness" of his only begotten Son (Ephesians 1:23).

Let the Christian, then, so regulate his prayers as to make them common, and embrace all who are his brethren in Christ; not only those whom at present he sees and knows to be such, but all men who are alive upon the earth. What God has determined with regard to them is beyond our knowledge, but to wish and hope the best concerning them is both pious and humane. Still it becomes us to regard with special affection those who are of the household of faith, and whom the Apostle has in express terms recommended to our care in everything (Galatians 6:10). In short, all our prayers ought to bear reference to that community which our Lord has established in his kingdom and family.

CHAPTER 39

*• We may pray specially for ourselves and certain others, provided
we have in our mind a general reference to all.*

This, however, does not prevent us from praying specially for ourselves, and certain others, provided our mind is not withdrawn from the view of this community, does not deviate from it, but constantly refers to it. For prayers, though couched in special terms, keeping that object still in view, cease not to be common.

All this may easily be understood by analogy. There is a general command from God to relieve the necessities of all the poor, and yet this command is obeyed by those who with that view give succor to all whom they see or know to be in distress, although they pass by many whose wants are not less urgent, either because they cannot know or are unable to give supply to all. In this way there is nothing repugnant to the will of God in those who, giving heed to this common society of the Church, yet offer up particular prayers, in which, with a public mind, though in special terms, they commend to God themselves or others, with whose necessity he has been pleased to make them more familiarly acquainted. It is true that prayer and the giving of our substance are not in all respects alike. We can only bestow the kindness of our liberality on those of whose wants we are aware, whereas in prayer we can assist the greatest strangers, how wide soever the space which may separate them from us.

This is done by that general form of prayer which, including all the sons of God, includes them also. To this we may refer the exhortation which Paul gave to the believers of his age, to lift up "holy hands without wrath and doubting" (1 Timothy 2:8). By reminding them that dissension is a bar to prayer, he shows it to be his wish that they should with one accord present their prayers in common.

CHAPTER 40

- *In what sense is God said to be in heaven?*

- *A threefold use of this doctrine for our consolation.*

- *Summary of the preface to the Lord's Prayer.*

The next words are, WHICH ART IN HEAVEN. From this we are not to infer that he is enclosed and confined within the circumference of heaven, as by a kind of boundaries. Hence Solomon confesses, "The heaven of heavens cannot contain thee" (1 Kings 8:27); and he himself says by the Prophet, "The heaven is my throne, and the earth is my footstool" (Isaiah 56:1); thereby intimating, that his presence, not confined to any region, is diffused over all space. But as our gross minds are unable to conceive of his ineffable glory, it is designated to us by heaven, nothing which our eyes can behold being so full of splendor and majesty. While, then, we are accustomed to regard every object as confined to the place where our senses discern it, no place can be assigned to God; and hence, if we would seek him, we must rise higher than all corporeal or mental discernment. Again, this form of expression reminds us that he is far beyond the reach of change or corruption, that he holds the whole universe in his grasp, and rules it by his power. The effect of the expressions therefore, is the same as if it had been said, that he is of infinite majesty, incomprehensible essence, boundless power, and eternal duration. When we thus speak of God, our thoughts must be raised to their highest pitch; we must not ascribe to him anything of a terrestrial or carnal nature, must not measure him by our little standards, or suppose his will to be like ours.

At the same time, we must put our confidence in him, understanding that heaven and earth are governed by his providence and power. In short, under the name of Father is set before us that God, who hath appeared to us in his own image, that we may invoke him with sure faith; the familiar name of Father being given not only to inspire confidence, but also to curb our minds, and prevent them from going astray after doubtful or fictitious gods. We thus ascend from the only begotten Son to the supreme Father of angels and of the Church. Then when his throne is fixed in heaven, we are reminded that he governs the world, and, therefore, that it is not in vain to approach him whose present care we actually experience. "He that cometh to God," says the Apostle, "must believe that he is, and that he is a rewarder of them that diligently seek him" (Hebrews 11:6). Here Christ makes both claims for his Father, first, that we place our faith in him; and, secondly, that we feel assured that our salvation is not neglected by him, inasmuch as he condescends to extend his providence to us.

By these elementary principles Paul prepares us to pray aright; for before enjoining us to make our requests known unto God, he premises in this way, "The Lord is at hand. Be careful for nothing" (Philippians 4:5, 6). Whence it appears that doubt and perplexity hang over the prayers of those in whose minds the belief is not firmly seated, that "the eyes of the Lord are upon the righteous" (Psalm 34:15).

CHAPTER 41

- *The necessity of the first petition as a proof of our unrighteousness.*

- *What is meant by the name of God and how it is hallowed?*

- *The sins by which the name of God is profaned.*

The first petition is, HALLOWED BE THY NAME. The necessity of presenting it bespeaks our great disgrace. For what can be more unbecoming than that our ingratitude and malice should impair, our audacity and petulance should as much as in them lies destroy, the glory of God? But though all the ungodly should burst with sacrilegious rage, the holiness of God's name still shines forth. Justly does the Psalmist exclaim, "According to thy name, O God, so is thy praise unto the ends of the earth" (Psalm 48:10). For wherever God hath made himself known, his perfections must be displayed, his power, goodness, wisdom, justice, mercy, and truth, which fill us with admiration, and incite us to show forth his praise. Therefore, as the name of God is not duly hallowed on the earth, and we are otherwise unable to assert it, it is at least our duty to make it the subject of our prayers. The sum of the whole is, It must be our desire that God may receive the honor which is his due: that men may never think or speak of him without the greatest reverence. The opposite of this reverence is profanity, which has always been too common in the world, and is very prevalent in the present day.

Hence the necessity of the petition, which, if piety had any proper existence among us, would be superfluous. But if the name of God is duly hallowed only when separated from all other names it alone is glorified, we are in the petition enjoined to ask not only that God would vindicate his sacred name from all contempt and insult, but also that he would compel the whole human race to reverence it. Then since God manifests himself to us partly by his word, and partly by his works, he is not sanctified unless in regard to both of these we ascribe to him what is due, and thus embrace whatever has proceeded from him, giving no less praise to his justice than to his mercy. On the manifold diversity of his works he has inscribed the marks of his glory, and these ought to call forth from every tongue an ascription of praise.

Thus Scripture will obtain its due authority with us, and no event will hinder us from celebrating the praises of God, in regard to every part of his government. On the other hand, the petition implies a wish that all impiety which pollutes this sacred name may perish and be extinguished, that everything which obscures or impairs his glory, all detraction and insult, may cease; that all blasphemy being suppressed, the divine majesty may be more and more signally displayed.

CHAPTER 42

- *The distinction between the first and second petitions.*

- *The advent of the kingdom of God in the world.*

The second petition is, THY KINGDOM COME. This contains nothing new, and yet there is good reason for distinguishing it from the first. For if we consider our lethargy in the greatest of all matters, we shall see how necessary it is that what ought to be in itself perfectly known should be inculcated at greater length. Therefore, after the injunction to pray that God would reduce to order, and at length completely efface every stain which is thrown on his sacred name, another petition, containing almost the same wish, is added, viz., Thy kingdom come.

Although a definition of this kingdom has already been given, I now briefly repeat that God reigns when men, in denial of themselves and contempt of the world and this earthly life, devote themselves to righteousness and aspire to heaven (Matthew 6). Thus this kingdom consists of two parts; the first is, when God by the agency of his Spirit corrects all the depraved lusts of the flesh, which in bands war against Him; and the second, when he brings all our thoughts into obedience to his authority. This petition, therefore, is duly presented only by those who begin with themselves; in other words, who pray that they may be purified from all the corruptions which disturb the tranquility and impair the purity of God's kingdom. Then as the word of God is like his royal scepter, we are here enjoined to pray that he would subdue all minds and hearts to voluntary obedience. This is done when by the secret inspiration of his Spirit he displays the efficacy of his word, and raises it to the place of honor which it deserves. We must next descend to the wicked, who perversely and with desperate madness resist his authority.

God, therefore, sets up his kingdom, by humbling the whole world, though in different ways, taming the wantonness of some, and breaking the ungovernable pride of others. We should desire this to be done every day, in order that God may gather churches to himself from all quarters of the world, may extend and increase their numbers, enrich them with his gifts, establish due order among them; on the other hand, beat down all the enemies of pure doctrine and religion, dissipate their counsels, defeat their attempts.

Hence it appears that there is good ground for the precept which enjoins daily progress, for human affairs are never so prosperous as when the impurities of vice are purged away, and integrity flourishes in full vigor. The completion, however, is deferred to the final advent of Christ, when, as Paul declares, "God will be all in all" (1 Corinthians 15:28). This prayer, therefore, ought to withdraw us from the corruptions of the world which separate us from God, and prevent his kingdom from flourishing within us; secondly, it ought to inflame us with an ardent desire for the mortification of the flesh; and, lastly, it ought to train us to the endurance of the cross; since this is the way in which God would have his kingdom to be advanced. It ought not to grieve us that the outward man decays provided the inner man is renewed. For such is the nature of the kingdom of God, that while we submit to his righteousness he makes us partakers of his glory. This is the case when continually adding to his light and truth, by which the lies and the darkness of Satan and his kingdom are dissipated, extinguished, and destroyed, he protects his people, guides them aright by the agency of his Spirit, and confirms them in perseverance; while, on the other hand, he frustrates the impious conspiracies of his enemies, dissipates their wiles and frauds, prevents their malice and curbs their petulance, until at length he consume Antichrist "with the spirit of his mouth," and destroy all impiety "with the brightness of his coming" (2 Thessalonians 2:8).

CHAPTER 43

- *Distinction between the second and third petitions.*

- *Conclusion of the three first petitions.*

The third petition is, THY WILL BE DONE ON EARTH AS IT IS IN HEAVEN. Though this depends on his kingdom, and cannot be disjoined from it, yet a separate place is not improperly given to it on account of our ignorance, which does not at once or easily apprehend what is meant by God reigning in the world. This, therefore, may not improperly be taken as the explanation, that God will be King in the world when all shall subject themselves to his will. We are not here treating of that secret will by which he governs all things, and destines them to their end. For although devils and men rise in tumult against him, he is able by his incomprehensible counsel not only to turn aside their violence, but make it subservient to the execution of his decrees. What we here speak of is another will of God, namely, that of which voluntary obedience is the counterpart; and, therefore, heaven is expressly contrasted with earth, because, as is said in The Psalms, the angels "do his commandments, hearkening unto the voice of his word" (Psalm 103:20).

We are, therefore, enjoined to pray that as everything done in heaven is at the command of God, and the angels are calmly disposed to do all that is right, so the earth may be brought under his authority, all rebellion and depravity having been extinguished. In presenting this request we renounce the desires of the flesh, because he who does not entirely resign his affections to God, does as much as in him lies to oppose the divine will, since everything which proceeds from us is vicious. Again, by this prayer we are taught to deny ourselves, that God may rule us according to his pleasure; and not only so, but also having annihilated our own may create new thoughts and new minds so that we shall have no desire save that of entire agreement with his will; in short, wish nothing of ourselves, but have our hearts governed by his Spirit, under whose inward teaching we may learn to love those things which please and hate those things which displease him.

Hence also we must desire that he would nullify and suppress all affections which are repugnant to his will. Such are the three first heads of the prayer, in presenting which we should have the glory of God only in view, taking no account of ourselves, and paying no respect to our own advantage, which, though it is thereby greatly promoted, is not here to be the subject of request. And though all the events prayed for must happen in their own time, without being either thought of, wished, or asked by us, it is still our duty to wish and ask for them. And it is of no slight importance to do so, that we may testify and profess that we are the servants and children of God, desirous by every means in our power to promote the honor due to him as our Lord and Father, and truly and thoroughly devoted to his service.

Hence if men, in praying that the name of God may be hallowed, that his kingdom may come, and his will be done, are not influenced by this zeal for the promotion of his glory, they are not to be accounted among the servants and children of God; and as all these things will take place against their will, so they will turn out to their confusion and destruction.

CHAPTER 44

- *A summary of the second part of the Lord's Prayer.*

- *What is meant by "bread."*

- *Why the petition for bread precedes that for the forgiveness of sins.*

- *Why this is to be sought daily.*

- *The doctrine resulting from this petition illustrated by an example.*

- *Two classes of men sin in regard to this petition.*

- *In what sense it is called, "our" bread.*

- *Why we ask God to give it to us.*

Now comes the second part of the prayer, in which we descend to our own interests, not, indeed, that we are to lose sight of the glory of God (to which, as Paul declares, we must have respect even in meat and drink, 1 Corinthians 10:31), and ask only what is expedient for ourselves; but the distinction, as we have already observed, is this: God claiming the three first petitions as specially his own, carries us entirely to himself, that in this way he may prove our piety.

Next he permits us to look to our own advantage, but still on the condition, that when we ask anything for ourselves it must be in order that all the benefits which he confers may show forth his glory, there being nothing more incumbent on us than to live and die to him. By the first petition of the second part, GIVE US THIS DAY OUR DAILY BREAD, we pray in general that God would give us all things which the body requires in this sublunary state, not only food and clothing, but everything which he knows will assist us to eat our bread in peace. In this way we briefly cast our care upon him, and commit ourselves to his providence, that he may feed, foster, and preserve us. For our heavenly Father disdains not to take our body under his charge and protection, that he may exercise our faith in those minute matters, while we look to him for everything, even to a morsel of bread and a drop of water. For since, owing to some strange inequality, we feel more concern for the body than for the soul, many who can trust the latter to God still continue anxious about the former, still hesitate as to what they are to eat, as to how they are to be clothed, and are in trepidation whenever their hands are not filled with corn, and wine, and oil (Psalm 4:8): so much more value do we set on this shadowy, fleeting life, than on a blessed immortality.

But those who, trusting to God, have once cast away that anxiety about the flesh, immediately look to him for greater gifts, even salvation and eternal life. It is no slight exercise of faith, therefore, to hope in God for things which would otherwise give us so much concern; nor have we made little progress when we get quit of this unbelief, which cleaves, as it were, to our very bones. The speculations of some concerning supersubstantial bread seem to be very little accordant with our Savior's meaning; for our prayer would be defective were we not to ascribe to God the nourishment even of this fading life. The reason which they give is heathenish, viz., that it is inconsistent with the character of sons of God, who ought to be spiritual, not only to occupy their mind with earthly cares, but to suppose God also occupied with them. As if his blessing and paternal favor were not eminently displayed in giving us food, or as if there were nothing in the declaration that godliness hath "the promise of the life that now is, and of that which is to come" (1 Timothy 4:8).

But although the forgiveness of sins is of far more importance than the nourishment of the body, yet Christ has set down the inferior in the prior place, in order that he might gradually raise us to the other two petitions, which properly belong to the heavenly life, -- in this providing for our sluggishness. We are enjoined to ask our bread, that we may be contented with the measure which our heavenly Father is pleased to dispense, and not strive to make gain by illicit arts.

Meanwhile, we must hold that the title by which it is ours is donation, because, as Moses says (Leviticus 26:20, Deuteronomy 8:17), neither our industry, nor labor, nor hands, acquire anything for us, unless the blessing of God be present; nay, not even would abundance of bread be of the least avail were it not divinely converted into nourishment. And hence this liberality of God is not less necessary to the rich than the poor, because, though their cellars and barns were full, they would be parched and pine with want did they not enjoy his favor along with their bread. The terms this day, or, as it is in another Evangelist, daily, and also the epithet daily, lay a restraint on our immoderate desire of fleeting good -- a desire which we are extremely apt to indulge to excess, and from which other evils ensue: for when our supply is in richer abundance we ambitiously squander it in pleasure, luxury, ostentation, or other kinds of extravagance.

Wherefore, we are only enjoined to ask as much as our necessity requires, and as it were for each day, confiding that our heavenly Father, who gives us the supply of to-day, will not fail us on the morrow. How great soever our abundance may be, however well filled our cellars and granaries, we must still always ask for daily bread, for we must feel assured that all substance is nothing, unless in so far as the Lord, by pouring out his blessing, make it fruitful during its whole progress; for even that which is in our hand is not ours except in so far as he every hour portions it out, and permits us to use it. As nothing is more difficult to human pride than the admission of this truth, the Lord declares that he gave a special proof for all ages, when he fed his people with manna in the desert (Deuteronomy 8:3), that he might remind us that "man shall not live by bread alone, but by every word that proceedeth out of the mouth of God" (Matthew 4:4). It is thus intimated, that by his power alone our life and strength are sustained, though he ministers supply to us by bodily instruments. In like manner, whenever it so pleases, he gives us a proof of an opposite description, by breaking the strength, or, as he himself calls it, the staff of bread (Leviticus 26:26), and leaving us even while eating to pine with hunger, and while drinking to be parched with thirst. Those who, not contented with daily bread, indulge an unrestrained insatiable cupidity, or those who are full of their own abundance, and trust in their own riches, only mock God by offering up this prayer.

For the former ask what they would be unwilling to obtain, nay, what they most of all abominate, namely, daily bread only, and as much as in them lies disguise their avarice from God, whereas true prayer should pour out the whole soul and every inward feeling before him. The latter, again, ask what they do not at all expect to obtain, namely, what they imagine that they in themselves already possess. In its being called ours, God, as we have already said, gives a striking display of his kindness, making that to be ours to which we have no just claim. Nor must we reject the view to which I have already adverted, viz., that this name is given to what is obtained by just and honest labor, as contrasted with what is obtained by fraud and rapine, nothing being our own which we obtain with injury to others. When we ask God to give us, the meaning is, that the thing asked is simply and freely the gift of God, whatever be the quarter from which it comes to us, even when it seems to have been specially prepared by our own art and industry, and procured by our hands, since it is to his blessing alone that all our labors owe their success.

CHAPTER 45

- *The close connection between this and the subsequent petition.*

- *Why our sins are called debts.*

- *This petition is violated:*

    a. *By those who think they can satisfy God by their own merits, or those of others.*

    b. *By those who dream of a perfection which makes pardon unnecessary.*

- *Why the elect cannot attain perfection in this life and a refutation of the libertine dreamers of perfection.*

- *In what sense we are said to forgive those who have sinned against us? How this condition is to be understood.*

The next petition is, FORGIVE US OUR DEBTS. In this and the following petition our Savior has briefly comprehended whatever is conducive to the heavenly life, as these two members contain the spiritual covenant which God made for the salvation of his Church, "I will put my law in their inward parts, and write it on their hearts." "I will pardon all their iniquities" (Jeremiah 31:33; 33:8).

Here our Savior begins with the forgiveness of sins, and then adds the subsequent blessing, viz., that God would protect us by the power, and support us by the aid of his Spirit, so that we may stand invincible against all temptations. To sins he gives the name of debts, because we owe the punishment due to them, a debt which we could not possibly pay were we not discharged by this remission, the result of his free mercy, when he freely expunges the debt, accepting nothing in return; but of his own mercy receiving satisfaction in Christ, who gave himself a ransom for us (Romans 3:24).

Hence, those who expect to satisfy God by merits of their own or of others, or to compensate and purchase forgiveness by means of satisfactions, have no share in this free pardon, and while they address God in this petition, do nothing more than subscribe their own accusation, and seal their condemnation by their own testimony. For they confess that they are debtors, unless they are discharged by means of forgiveness. This forgiveness, however, they do not receive, but rather reject, when they obtrude their merits and satisfactions upon God, since by so doing they do not implore his mercy, but appeal to his justice.

Let those, again, who dream of a perfection which makes it unnecessary to seek pardon, find their disciples among those whose itching ears incline them to imposture[25], (see Calvin on Daniel 9:20); only let them understand that those whom they thus acquire have been carried away from Christ, since he, by instructing all to confess their guilt, receives none but sinners, not that he may soothe, and so encourage them in their sins, but because he knows that believers are never so divested of the sins of the flesh as not to remain subject to the justice of God. It is, indeed, to be wished, it ought even to be our strenuous endeavor, to perform all the parts of our duty, so as truly to congratulate ourselves before God as being pure from every stain; but as God is pleased to renew his image in us by degrees, so that to some extent there is always a residue of corruption in our flesh, we ought by no means to neglect the remedy.

But if Christ, according to the authority given him by his Father, enjoins us, during the whole course of our lives, to implore pardon, who can tolerate those new teachers who, by the phantom of perfect innocence, endeavor to dazzle the simple, and make them believe that they can render themselves completely free from guilt? This, as John declares, is nothing else than to make God a liar (1 John 1:10). In like manner, those foolish men mutilate the covenant in which we have seen that our salvation is contained by concealing one head of it, and so destroying it entirely; being guilty not only of profanity in that they separate things which ought to be indissolubly connected; but

---

[25] French, "Telles disciples qu'ils voudront;"--such disciples as they will.

also of wickedness and cruelty in overwhelming wretched souls with despair -- of treachery also to themselves and their followers, in that they encourage themselves in a carelessness diametrically opposed to the mercy of God. It is excessively childish to object, that when they long for the advent of the kingdom of God, they at the same time pray for the abolition of sin. In the former division of the prayer absolute perfection is set before us; but in the latter our own weakness.

Thus the two fitly correspond to each other -- we strive for the goal, and at the same time neglect not the remedies which our necessities require. In the next part of the petition we pray to be forgiven, "as we forgive our debtors;" that is, as we spare and pardon all by whom we are in any way offended, either in deed by unjust, or in word by contumelious treatment. Not that we can forgive the guilt of a fault or offence; this belongs to God only; but we can forgive to this extent: we can voluntarily divest our minds of wrath, hatred, and revenge, and efface the remembrance of injuries by a voluntary oblivion.

Wherefore, we are not to ask the forgiveness of our sins from God, unless we forgive the offenses of all who are or have been injurious to us. If we retain any hatred in our minds, if we meditate revenge, and devise the means of hurting; nay, if we do not return to a good understanding with our enemies, perform every kind of friendly office, and endeavor to effect a reconciliation with them, we by this petition beseech God not to grant us forgiveness. For we ask him to do to us as we do to others. This is the same as asking him not to do unless we do also. What, then, do such persons obtain by this petition but a heavier judgment?

Lastly, it is to be observed that the condition of being forgiven as we forgive our debtors, is not added because by forgiving others we deserve forgiveness, as if the cause of forgiveness were expressed; but by the use of this expression the Lord has been pleased partly to solace the weakness of our faith, using it as a sign to assure us that our sins are as certainly forgiven as we are certainly conscious of having forgiven others, when our mind is completely purged from all envy, hatred, and malice; and partly using as a badge by which he excludes from the number of his children all who, prone to revenge and reluctant to forgive, obstinately keep up their enmity, cherishing against others that indignation which they deprecate from themselves; so that they should not venture to invoke him as a Father. In the Gospel of Luke, we have this distinctly stated in the words of Christ.

CHAPTER 46

- *The sixth petition reduced to three points:*

  a. *The various forms of temptation. The depraved conceptions of our minds. The wiles of Satan, on the right hand and on the left. 2.*

  b. *What it is to be led into temptation. We do not ask not to be tempted of God.*

  c. *What meant by evil, or the evil one.*

- *Summary of this petition: How necessary it is; condemns the pride of the superstitious; includes many excellent properties.*

- *In what sense may God be said to lead us into temptation?*

The sixth petition corresponds (as we have observed) to the promise[26] of writing the law upon our hearts; but because we do not obey God without a continual warfare, without sharp and arduous contests, we here pray that he would furnish us with armor, and defend us by his protection, that we may be able to obtain the victory.

By this we are reminded that we not only have need of the gift of the Spirit inwardly to soften our hearts, and turn and direct them to the obedience of God, but also of his assistance, to render us invincible by all the wiles and violent assaults of Satan. The forms of temptation are many and various. The depraved conceptions of our minds provoking us to transgress the law -- conceptions which our concupiscence suggests or the devil excites, are temptations; and things which in their own nature are not evil, become temptations by the wiles of the devil, when they are presented to our eyes in such a way that the view

---

[26] The French adds, "que Dieu nous a donnee et faite;"--which God has given and performed to us.

of them makes us withdraw or decline from God[27]. These temptations are both on the right hand and on the left[28].

On the right, when riches, power, and honors, which by their glare, and the semblance of good which they present, generally dazzle the eyes of men, and so entice by their blandishments, that, caught by their snares, and intoxicated by their sweetness, they forget their God: on the left, when offended by the hardship and bitterness of poverty, disgrace, contempt, afflictions, and other things of that description, they despond, cast away their confidence and hope, and are at length totally estranged from God.

In regard to both kinds of temptation, which either enkindled in us by concupiscence, or presented by the craft of Satan's war against us, we pray God the Father not to allow us to be overcome, but rather to raise and support us by his hand, that strengthened by his mighty power we may stand firm against all the assaults of our malignant enemy, whatever be the thoughts which he sends into our minds; next we pray that whatever of either description is allotted us, we may turn to good, that is, may neither be inflated with prosperity, nor cast down by adversity. Here, however, we do not ask to be altogether exempted from temptation, which is very necessary to excite, stimulate, and urge us on, that we may not become too lethargic. It was not without reason that David wished to be tried[29], nor is it without cause that the Lord daily tries his elect, chastising them by disgrace, poverty, tribulation, and other kinds of cross[30].

But the temptations of God and Satan are very different: Satan tempts, that he may destroy, condemn, confound, throw headlong; God, that by proving his people he may make trial of their sincerity,

---

[27] James 1:2, 14; Matth. 4:1, 3; 1 Thess. 3:5.

[28] 2 Cor. 6:7, 8.

[29] Ps. 26:2.

[30] Gen. 22:1; Deut. 8:2; 13:3. For the sense in which God is said to lead us into temptation, see the end of this section.

and by exercising their strength confirm it; may mortify, tame, and cauterize their flesh, which, if not curbed in this manner, would wanton and exult above measure. Besides, Satan attacks those who are unarmed and unprepared, that he may destroy them unawares; whereas whatever God sends, he "will with the temptation also make a way to escape, that ye may be able to bear it[31]." Whether by the term evil we understand the devil or sin, is not of the least consequence. Satan is indeed the very enemy who lays snares for our life[32], but it is by sin that he is armed for our destruction.

Our petition, therefore, is, that we may not be overcome or overwhelmed with temptation, but in the strength of the Lord may stand firm against all the powers by which we are assailed; in other words, may not fall under temptation: that being thus taken under his charge and protection, we may remain invincible by sin, death, the gates of hell, and the whole power of the devil; in other words, be delivered from evil. Here it is carefully to be observed, that we have no strength to contend with such a combatant as the devil, or to sustain the violence of his assault. Were it otherwise, it would be mockery of God to ask of him what we already possess in ourselves.

Assuredly those who in self-confidence prepare for such a fight, do not understand how bold and well-equipped the enemy is with whom they have to do. Now we ask to be delivered from his power, as from the mouth of some furious raging lion, who would instantly tear us with his teeth and claws, and swallow us up, did not the Lord rescue us from the midst of death; at the same time knowing that if the Lord is present and will fight for us while we stand by, through him "we shall do valiantly" (Psalm 60:12). Let others if they will confide in the powers and resources of their free will which they think they possess; enough for us that we stand and are strong in the power of God alone. But the prayer comprehends more than at first sight it seems to do. For if the Spirit of God is our strength in waging the contest

---

[31] 1 Cor. 10:13; 2 Pet. 2:92 Pet. 2:9.

[32] 1 Pet. 5:8.

with Satan, we cannot gain the victory unless we are filled with him, and thereby freed from all infirmity of the flesh. Therefore, when we pray to be delivered from sin and Satan, we at the same time desire to be enriched with new supplies of divine grace, until completely replenished with them, we triumph over every evil.

To some it seems rude and harsh to ask God not to lead us into temptation, since, as James declares (James 1:13), it is contrary to his nature to do so. This difficulty has already been partly solved by the fact that our concupiscence is the cause, and therefore properly bears the blame of all the temptations by which we are overcome. All that James means is, that it is vain and unjust to ascribe to God vices which our own consciousness compels us to impute to ourselves.

But this is no reason why God may not when he sees it meet bring us into bondage to Satan, give us up to a reprobate mind and shameful lusts, and so by a just, indeed, but often hidden judgment, lead us into temptation. Though the cause is often concealed from men, it is well known to him. Hence we may see that the expression is not improper, if we are persuaded that it is not without cause he so often threatens to give sure signs of his vengeance, by blinding the reprobate, and hardening their hearts.

CHAPTER 47

- *The three final petitions show that the prayers of Christians ought to be public.*

- *The conclusion of the Lord's Prayer.*

- *Why the word "Amen" is added.*

These three petitions, in which we specially commend ourselves and all that we have to God, clearly show what we formerly observed (chapters 38, 39), that the prayers of Christians should be public, and have respect to the public edification of the Church and the advancement of believers in spiritual communion. For no one requests that anything should be given to him as an individual, but we all ask in common for daily bread and the forgiveness of sins, not to be led into temptation, but delivered from evil.

Moreover, there is subjoined the reason for our great boldness in asking and confidence of obtaining (chapters 11, 36). Although this does not exist in the Latin copies, yet as it accords so well with the whole, we cannot think of omitting it. The words are, THINE IS THE KINGDOM, AND THE POWER, AND THE GLORY, FOR EVER. Here is the calm and firm assurance of our faith. For were our prayers to be commended to God by our own worth, who would venture even to whisper before him? Now, however wretched we may be, however unworthy, however devoid of commendation, we shall never want a reason for prayer, nor a ground of confidence, since the kingdom, power, and glory, can never be wrested from our Father.

The last word is AMEN, by which is expressed the eagerness of our desire to obtain the things which we ask, while our hope is confirmed, that all things have already been obtained and will assuredly be granted to us, seeing they have been promised by God, who cannot deceive. This accords with the form of expression to which we have already adverted: "Grant, O Lord, for thy name's sake, not on account of us or of our righteousness." By this the saints not only express the end of their prayers, but confess that they are unworthy of obtaining did not God find the cause in himself and were not their confidence founded entirely on his nature.

CHAPTER 48

- *The Lord's Prayer contains everything that we can or ought to ask of God.*

- *Those who go beyond it sin.*

All things that we ought, indeed all that we are able, to ask of God, are contained in this formula, and as it were rule, of prayer delivered by Christ, our divine Master, whom the Father has appointed to be our teacher, and to whom alone he would have us to listen (Matth. 17:5). For he ever was the eternal wisdom of the Father, and being made man, was manifested as the Wonderful, the Counselor (Isaiah 11:2; 9:6). Accordingly, this prayer is complete in all its parts, so complete, that whatever is extraneous and foreign to it, whatever cannot be referred to it, is impious and unworthy of the approbation of God. For he has here summarily prescribed what is worthy of him, what is acceptable to him, and what is necessary for us; in short, whatever he is pleased to grant.

Those, therefore, who presume to go further and ask something more from God, first seek to add of their own to the wisdom of God (this it is insane blasphemy to do); secondly, refusing to confine themselves within the will of God, and despising it, they wander as their cupidity directs; lastly, they will never obtain anything, seeing they pray without faith. For there cannot be a doubt that all such prayers are made without faith, because at variance with the word of God, on which if faith do not always lean it cannot possibly stand. Those who, disregarding the Master's rule, indulge their own wishes, not only have not the word of God, but as much as in them lies oppose it. Hence Tertullian (*De Fuga in Persecutione*) has not less truly than elegantly termed it Lawful Prayer, tacitly intimating that all other prayers are lawless and illicit.

CHAPTER 49

• We may, after the example of the saints, frame our prayers in different words, provided there is no difference in meaning.

By this, however, we would not have it understood that we are so restricted to this form of prayer as to make it unlawful to change a word or syllable of it. For in Scripture we meet with many prayers differing greatly from it in word, yet written by the same Spirit, and capable of being used by us with the greatest advantage. Many prayers also are continually suggested to believers by the same Spirit, though in expression they bear no great resemblance to it.

All we mean to say is, that no man should wish, expect, or ask anything which is not summarily comprehended in this prayer. Though the words may be very different, there must be no difference in the sense. In this way, all prayers, both those which are contained in the Scripture, and those which come forth from pious breasts, must be referred to it, certainly none can ever equal it, far less surpass it in perfection. It omits nothing which we can conceive in praise of God, nothing which we can imagine advantageous to man, and the whole is so exact that all hope of improving it may well be renounced. In short, let us remember that we have here the doctrine of heavenly wisdom. God has taught what he willed; he willed what was necessary.

CHAPTER 50

- *Circumstances to be observed.*

- *Appointing special hours of prayer.*

- *What is to be aimed at and what is to be avoided.*

- *The will of God governs our prayer.*

But although it has been said above (chapters 7, 27, etc.), that we ought always to raise our minds upwards towards God, and pray without ceasing, yet such is our weakness, which requires to be supported, such our torpor, which requires to be stimulated, that it is requisite for us to appoint special hours for this exercise, hours which are not to pass away without prayer, and during which the whole affections of our minds are to be completely occupied; namely, when we rise in the morning, before we commence our daily work, when we sit down to food, when by the blessing of God we have taken it, and when we retire to rest. This, however, must not be a superstitious observance of hours, by which, as it were, performing a task to God, we think we are discharged as to other hours; it should rather be considered as a discipline by which our weakness is exercised, and ever and anon stimulated. In particular, it must be our anxious care, whenever we are ourselves pressed, or see others pressed by any strait, instantly to have recourse to him not only with quickened pace, but with quickened minds; and again, we must not in any prosperity of ourselves or others omit to testify our recognition of his hand by praise and thanksgiving.

Lastly, we must in all our prayers carefully avoid wishing to confine God to certain circumstances, or prescribe to him the time, place, or mode of action. In like manner, we are taught by this prayer not to fix any law or impose any condition upon him, but leave it entirely to him to adopt whatever course of procedure seems to him best, in respect of method, time, and place. For before we offer up any petition for ourselves, we ask that his will may be done, and by so doing place our will in subordination to his, just as if we had laid a curb upon it, that, instead of presuming to give law to God, it may regard him as the ruler and disposer of all its wishes.

CHAPTER 51

- *Perseverance in prayer is especially recommended, both by precept and example.*

- *Exhortation to those who assign to God a limited time and mode of hearing.*

If, with minds thus framed to obedience, we allow ourselves to be governed by the laws of Divine Providence, we shall easily learn to persevere in prayer, and suspending our own desires wait patiently for the Lord, certain, however little the appearance of it may be, that he is always present with us, and will in his own time show how very far he was from turning a deaf ear to prayers, though to the eyes of men they may seem to be disregarded. This will be a very present consolation, if at any time God does not grant an immediate answer to our prayers, preventing us from fainting or giving way to despondency, as those are wont to do who, in invoking God, are so borne away by their own fervor, that unless he yield on their first importunity and give present help, they immediately imagine that he is angry and offended with them and abandoning all hope of success cease from prayer. On the contrary, deferring our hope with well tempered equanimity, let us insist with that perseverance which is so strongly recommended to us in Scripture. We may often see in The Psalms how David and other believers, after they are almost weary of praying, and seem to have been beating the air by addressing a God who would not hear, yet cease not to pray because due authority is not given to the word of God, unless the faith placed in it is superior to all events.

Again, let us not tempt God, and by wearying him with our importunity provoke his anger against us. Many have a practice of formally bargaining with God on certain conditions, and, as if he were the servant of their lust, binding him to certain stipulations; with which if he do not immediately comply, they are indignant and fretful, murmur, complain, and make a noise. Thus offended, he often in his anger grants to such persons what in mercy he kindly denies to others. Of this we have a proof in the children of Israel, for whom it had been better not to have been heard by the Lord, than to swallow his indignation with their flesh (Numbers 11:18, 33).

CHAPTER 52

- *The dignity of faith, through which we always obtain,
  in answer to prayer, whatever is most expedient for us.*

- *The necessity of knowing this.*

But if our sense is not able till after long expectation to perceive what the result of prayer is, or experience any benefit from it, still our faith will assure us of that which cannot be perceived by sense, viz., that we have obtained what was fit for us, the Lord having so often and so surely engaged to take an interest in all our troubles from the moment they have been deposited in his bosom. In this way we shall possess abundance in poverty, and comfort in affliction. For though all things fail, God will never abandon us, and he cannot frustrate the expectation and patience of his people. He alone will suffice for all, since in himself he comprehends all good, and will at last reveal it to us on the day of judgment, when his kingdom shall be plainly manifested.

We may add, that although God complies with our request, he does not always give an answer in the very terms of our prayers but while apparently holding us in suspense, yet in an unknown way, shows that our prayers have not been in vain. This is the meaning of the words of John, "If we know that he hear us, whatsoever we ask, we know that we have the petitions that we desired of him" (1 John 5:15). It might seem that there is here a great superfluity of words, but the declaration is most useful, namely, that God, even when he does not comply with our requests, yet listens and is favorable to our prayers, so that our hope founded on his word is never disappointed. But believers have always need of being supported by this patience, as they could not stand long if they did not lean upon it. For the trials by which the Lord proves and exercises us are severe, nay, he often drives us to extremes, and when driven allows us long to stick fast in the mire before he gives us any taste of his sweetness. As Hannah says, "The Lord killeth, and maketh alive; he bringeth down to the grave, and bringeth up" (1 Samuel 2:6). What could they here do but become dispirited and rush on despair, were they not, when afflicted, desolate, and half dead, comforted with the thought that they are regarded by God, and that there will be an end to their present evils. But however secure their hopes may stand, they in the meantime cease not to pray, since prayer unaccompanied by perseverance leads to no result.